POETRY
FOR THE
NOW
2

JOHAN LEWIS

Poetry for the Now 2
Copyright © 2014 Johan Lewis. All rights reserved.
ISBN 978-1-312-01838-9

With the exception of pages 13 and 21, all illustrations including the front and back cover are © 2014 Wilson Tanner. Illustrations on pages 13 and 21 are ©2014 Bradley F. Edwards. Please visit wtanner.com and bradleyfedwards.com for more equally impressive artwork.

No part of this book may be used or reproduced by any means: graphic, electronic, or mechanical, including photocopying, recording, taping or by simply saying parts of the book aloud in public places where more than two people are present. All public readings of this book, while surely in high demand, must be performed without the use of microphones, overhead projectors, or visual aids of any kind. If somehow a miracle drops from the sky and the author allows any public reading of this book, the speaker shall be allowed one microphone, and the level of the volume shall be set no higher than 7.

The views expressed in this work are solely those of the author. Because of the very nature of an 'idea,' it almost goes without saying that those expressed here do not necessarily reflect the views of the publisher, because the publisher and the author are two separate entities in this vast universe, and the confluence of experience gathered by each of them subjectively could not possibly be exactly the same, simply because the author is pretty sure that he and the publisher did not grow up in the same town, being that the author knew pretty much everyone and would have heard of someone named Lulu. In the event that the publisher is not a person named Lulu, and 'publisher' refers to instead a conglomerate of all different people who represent one unified viewpoint, well then, the author would like to chuckle at the very idea, for if two people cannot share the exact same viewpoint, how could an entire bevy of them? In any case, the publisher (whoever he/she/they is/are) hereby disclaims any responsibility for them.

DISCLAIMER: This book contains moments of illumination that, when experienced, are equivalent to the violent flashes of a strobe light, so those with heart conditions are hereby forewarned to keep a glass of tepid milk by their side as they read, and as soon as glimpses of nirvana start to appear on the distant horizons of the psyche, are hereby advised to drop the book on the floor and throw the glass of milk at the nearest pet or child. The sudden physical comedy that arises should shake them out of their reverie and all should be right as rain again. The author and publisher hereby disclaim any responsibility for the cleaning up of any milk in living rooms across the world.

For all the dreamers' realistic and disapproving parents.

I SMELL A DECENT OMELETTE

The dots, the dots!
Connect the dots
and create new shapes!
The lines take form and show me ponies,
or stars in the sky
or a nice blender.

But the dots, the dots!

What if they floated off the page
and spun around me
like pepper from an open palm?
What then?
What would the lines do
without the dots?

I'd be at my desk,
And looking down at the page,
I'd be all, like,
Who has the dots *now*, you fucking pony?

OBEY THE RESISTANCE OR PAY THE PRICE OF A BAR OF SOAP

When will the painting be complete,
monseigneur?
I pay you too well
to not know the status
of what will assuredly be
the next "Napoleon at Waterloo."

Four days?
Surely you jest.
I've been standing here
poised
with these watermelons under my arms
and this ostrich feather in my cap
balancing on this unicycle
for nearly five days now.

How have you not yet captured
my royal aura?

No, no more supplies for you.
The oils and brushes are sufficient.

You must needs calm down.
Your time is running short,
you lazy Frenchman.

Put down that bucket.
I order you to put down that bucket!

Hmph, no need for petty insults, sir,
I may be holding two melons
but I am still a nobleman.

There's a good lad.
Now, step away from the painting.
That's it.
A little further.
Little further.

Aha! Right into my pit of snakes!

LUCIFER, BARRABAS, AND THE PRINCE OF THIEVES

My God, you smell like something.
Let me take a guess.
You smell as if you just came
from your uncle's funeral
and leaned over the casket
and kissed his wrinkled head
and wept salty tears
and went to the wake
and then to the snack table
and then took a chip
and put (too much) guacamole on it
and spilled it on your blouse.

Am I right?

Oh, damn it.
I'm usually very good at this.
What did I get wrong?

Ah, I see.
It was your daughter's funeral,
Not your uncle's.

I'm very sorry to hear that.

Well, don't keep me in suspense here.
Was the guacamole
at least
any good?

IT'S THE THING THAT BROUGHT DOWN THE WALL

She puts the glasses over her thighs,
and tells me to bend down,
kiss her knees,
but look at her *other* eyes, and longingly, damn it.

I comply,
because I love her,
but I wish she'd wash her jeans, is all.

A SMIRK CAN SOMETIMES GO LONGER THAN A DRESS

Sometimes there is meaning
in the clouds.
Look over yonder, darling,
at that grouping to the left.
Does that not look like your Uncle Harry
kissing your Aunt Susan?

Mm.

And what of those, there?
Do those not resemble
your cousins
Timmy and Tammy
at their usual game
of hide the hammock?

Mm.

Ah, and glance upon that one!
That is certainly your mother
chiding me for finding that old
chestnut wardrobe
she thought she had hidden so well.
Oh, how she had wanted to
surprise us!

Mm?

Yes, I see your relatives everywhere.
Well, do they not resemble them?
Tell me that one there isn't
your second niece (once removed) Frank–

No, I do not see any
of my family
in the clouds.

Because they all died in the fire.
You know that.

Mm? Oh, did I never tell you that story?

ART AND FART

This,
the only thing I know how to do.

I hope that one day
I still haven't given up
and have produced
an impressive body of work
so that all other generations
can at least say
(once I've gone)
that no other man
ever made
as many guinea pig-shaped cookie jars
as that man did.

IS IT TOO LATE TO CHANGE TO THE SALAD?

Plucking out the feathers of this chicken
seems a bit cruel.
Couldn't we just
ask it again?

(sigh) All right.
Mr. Cluckles,
I'm the good cop here,
if you haven't noticed,
so you'll believe me when I tell you
that this is your last chance.
I'll ask you one more time:
where did you hide
the blueprints?

That's a fucking lie.

I'm sorry.
I tried to protect you.

Marcus? Who the hell is Marcus?

Pluck away, Jim.

WASH MY SQUARE

This park is teeming with life—
the jazz is soaring over and under our bare-chested bodies,
the songs noticeable, sweet, and distant.
The people have come from their dusty abodes
and are ready to live again.
A man with a clipboard pitches politics
and I want nothing to do with him.
Then sun is setting soon
and the jazz will die with it.
We will all go home to our respective beers
and will wake up hoping
that we can simply
do this again.

RAIDING PERSONAL GOALS WITH POSITIVE AFFIRMATION

The time for discussing is over,
Marv.
You had your chances o'plenty
back at the farm.
You could have gotten on that convoy
but instead you stuck with me.
You know that I love you for that,
But you made your choice.
You're with me to the end on this one.
So get on that damned cow,
and start riding,
because in five weeks' time
we'll be in Nebraska
and welcomed as heroes
for holding the world record
for longest cow ride.

[click] Marv!
I am not going to
fucking
say it again!

Get on that damned saddled cow!

MET-LIFE

I am leaning against
the inside
of a window
thirty-four stories above the distant concrete.

My nose is pressed firm,
flattened,
and I place my palms
up next to my ears
and do my best
elephant sound.

I can feel the brew-aw! Brew-aw!
Vibrating against the glass
and my breath is steaming a small oval
and I begin to really get into it
and I stomp
and wave my hands as if my youngling were threatened
and brew-aw! Brew-aw!

Brew-aw! Brew-aw!

And my arm is an elephant trunk now
and I'm no longer just a guy finding a bathroom,
and these new, giant ears are the proof
and becoming what I've really always wanted
and I turn
and the window blasts open
perhaps from my own desires
and I am sucked out
twisting and turning.
I flap my ears
and the twentieth floor
I flap my ears
and the seventh floor
I flap my arm
and the first and
have you ever seen an elephant fly?

I should have pretended to be a bird.

A LOVELY CLASSROOM

The purple displays
the fountains mighty
the rapturous delight
oh the sweet mercy!
oh the final blow!
the timely exit
the fanciful desires
the fallacious deep breaths
the sinewy muscles
the browning morals
the twist and the leper
the apple core in the baby's mouth
the tip-tapping of mice on the sill
the steering and veering to the center
the fame
the mighty wind
the random projects and free labor
the party and the pet name
the shoulder sling
oh the sugared mountains!
oh the peppered nipples!
oh the Savannah's revenge!
oh the structured settlement!

oh my spine!
oh my turpentine!
oh my spine!
oh my turpentine!

THE MOVIES

If you buy an animal's turd
and rub it on your face,
and then you exclaim
that you have shit on your face,
would you ask for your money back?

Me too.

CHECK MY PULSE. IS THERE A BEAT? HOW FUNKY IS THAT?

At long last,
the morning is ours!
no more wanting and waning and pining
for the eve of another night.
We have been cavorting and scheming
ever since we spied this morn two months ago
on the calendar on the castle wall.

It was beautiful and perfect.
Do you remember that, Samuel?
Do you remember me taking you by the hand
and promising you that
one day
those golden trees
and slanted lights
and chirping birds
would all be ours one day?
Do you remember, Samuel?

Oh, how long it took to put our plan
into action.
We were such young fools then.
Trial and error were our middle names.
It was all we could do to find the morning—
We once stormed a muggy afternoon,
laid siege to a cool evening,
took a battering ram to an arid 2am,
but this morning has long eluded us.

What was our secret this time, Samuel?
I don't even know how we landed here.
Was it your brave cunning?
Was it my cunning bravery?
Was it our braving cunnery?

I blinked my eyes and a thousand years passed
and thrust forward like earthworms from a slingshot
you and I broke the boundaries of time
and the colors!
hurtling through effervescent space
I held your hand and caught a glimpse eternal

before we landed with a *thunk* on this hill.

Look at the land, Samuel.
Look at how flat and peaceful and new it all appears.
It's as if the world
pulled its pants down
just for us.
In secret-like, in a closet,
at its cousin's house late at night
far after spin the bottle had gone too far.
Do you agree, Samuel?
Can you see the bottom-bosom of the earth?
Smiling sideways, all coy-like and fresh?

Samuel, if you're going to sleep,
at least don't snore.
It's rude,
and very unbecoming,
especially for such an esteemed
morning-conqueror as you.

Here, come now, wake up,
I brought sandwiches.

MY EX-GIRLFRIEND PLAYS THE BASSOON REALLY WELL

It is very hard to
embrace
art.
Especially
at the Met
where currently
they are exhibiting
experimental
cactus sculptures.

They have made the pricklies
using real pricklies!

CANAL ST.

Apologies to the board,
first and foremost,
for delivering the contract
in blue ink.
(Written in blue ink, that is.
I was not submerged in a vat of blue ink
whilst I delivered it.)

I know that thou considers
blue
to be the most
unprofessional
of all the colors.

Yet consider this,
distinguished members of the board.
Every company in this sector
(including, mind you, our fiercest competitors)
uses blank ink in their contracts.
What if we,
Shoddenheim, Foddenheim, Calypso, and Associates,
went against the grain?
What if we became known
as the firm with blue ink?
Did you ever consider
thee ever consider
thine heather cog sitter
shrine tether dog fitter
that a renegade
is exactly
what this town needs?

Ladies and gentleman of the board,
I implore you –
cut me down from this lemon tree
in the desert!
Leave me not for the vultures!
I can do better next time!
Do not ride away!
At least leave me my knife!
Do not rob me of my ingenuity!

Alright, ladies and gentleman of the board,
you may ride deftly into
the soft El Paso evening
and think you have seen the last
of old Blue Ink Nelson here,
(That is what they shall call me!
Olllllllld Blue Ink!
They will say.)
You may smugly think yourself
safe and warm in your beds
content with silencing
a rogue like me.
Yet cowardly you left the job
unfinishe,
and as I wriggle around this
tree,
I wear away these ropes,
and my determination and rage
will soon reap vengeance
upon your house!
A plague on your house!
Or at least a good t.p.'ing!
It may take me days
or weeks
but I will erode these times
and escape
and find you
and wake you up
and stand over you
and smile to know your end.

I snap to it, perhaps waking,
and I am still here,
and you ladies and gentlemen of the board
never left at all
but are here now
with pistols pointed at my face.

You ask me if I have any last words,
and I ask,
Have you ever read *An Occurrence at Owl Creek Bridge*?

TRY, TRY, FRY, SIGH, TRY AGAIN

The Pacific, oh the Pacific!

I, a babe in swaddling clothes
tossed from my father's arms into the roaring calm
the beautiful blue
floated like Moses up the coast
with a laurel of torment bequeathed to me
and the sand sneaking its way
into newborn crevasses
(oh how this excites me so–
the birth of new ideas!)
and the gulls floated high overhead
cawing at the new arrival of a treasured member
and the fish snapping at my padded tuccus
and I giggled with ignorant joy
as I drifted farther southwards.

The Pacific, oh the Pacific!

How it cradled my young blood
and thwarted away all the potential cancers!
It was destiny
that current strong and wispy
that careened me to the Murphy's Cave
and nestled me into place
where I found myself among
hundreds of other babies!

The Pacific, oh the Pacific!

We were stacked on top of one another
our tiny hands pushing tiny faces
a cacophony of babies crying and wailing
for lost mothers and fathers
babies pigeon-holed into Murphy's Cave
for a shuddered, shrouded, hidden purpose!

Nay, no bottle to be found!
Nought a rattle to spare
nor a crib to occupy–
only babies upon babies!

Upon babies!

We cried through the first night,
cold and stiff and salty,
yet true and gritty and chock-full of
authentic experience,
and neither the roar of the waves
nor the glow of the moon on the distant horizon
(our first night light)
could assuage our natural fears
of being alive and in the world at long last.
We grappled one another
and with nimble, underdeveloped digits
tried to tear the swaddling clothes off one another.

I was lucky enough enough to be
one of the last ones to arrive
as I bobbled against the pile
half on the shore
I was not a fighter.
Others were two, three babies deep
and were yelping for air all through the night.

The Pacific, oh the Pacific!

How the morning taught us much about
the resistance!

The nature of nature!
Murphy's Cave turned in an instant
from the oppressive baby pile
into a new home!
And as soon as we were comfy,
the tide came at sunrise
and whisked us all away
out with the sun
and we drifted into the real world.
We clutched each other's hands and feet
and learned to hold on
and as one giant baby raft
we traveled out farther and farther
and some of us were plucked away
by greedy pelicans.

Only now do I see
what our purpose was.

The Pacific, oh the Pacific!

When we reached the island
at sundown
our numbers had waned considerably
and the lucky
along with the strong
were better for it.

On the shore of the island
ankle deep
stood many people
wearing grass skirts
and faces painted white.
They glowed with open arms
hands held high at attention
unmoving
waiting for us.

Out of my baby peripheral
I could see my father
and he patiently waited
(as was custom)
for me to flounder towards him
and as the whitewash lapped me close
he scooped me up
as did the others
and held me sky high
to get his first
real
good look at me.

You have your mother's eyes,
he said,
and all the others echoed similar
compliments,
as was custom.

The Pacific, oh the Pacific!

The parents that were left
without their child
were granted life long rights
to slaughter any pelican they saw.
My father put his hand on the shoulders
of the mourning
and let each one
kiss me on the cheek
as was custom.

And after the feast,
after the fire had died down,
my father plopped me into his canoe
facing him
and began paddling
back towards the mainland.

He told me how proud he was of me
and introduced me
to my older sister
who had been waiting in the canoe
impatiently
and she stroked my forehead
called me little boy
and we all laughed
because this was certainly not custom.

Oh, the Pacific!

THE LONG AND ARDUOUS TASK OF CREATING A WORKING ENVIRONMENT

How long
can we keep this up,
Penelope?
Your parents are soon going to find out about us
and when they do
they will kill you
and in your absence
adopt me as their son.

Thing is, I hate your room.

CASTLES IN THE ANCIENT PAST, CLOUDS IN THE PRESENT FUTURE

Apparently there is something
incredibly wrong with the world–
a wrong that the world has never known
a wrong that Sam Cooke could not have predicted
nor would have wanted to.

The world was much simpler then,
wasn't it?
Apples fell from trees
and we ate them.
The songs on the radio meant something,
and we ate those, too.

Practically everything back then was edible, wasn't it?
I remember my dad telling me that when he was a boy
that he used to eat politics for hours on end,
then he'd eat young people's sense of morality,
then he'd *devour* what was then
a very cosmopolitan fashion sense.

He'd sit on his rocking chair,
and drink lemonade
eating prunes and Elvis music,
and nothing ever came up,
nothing ever rotted or spoiled
because there were no preservatives in any of it–
nothing caused cancer
because he used to eat cancer, too–
spreading it all over his toast
and licking it off the tips of his fingers.
He would eat vanity and death,
but never television!
For without getting too preachy,
television is the only thing
that was
and always will be
the original evil.

With the exception,
perhaps,
of *Frasier*.

PRESTIGE, SUNSHINE, AND A LARK

I am wearing a hat today,
a hat you've never seen
no I will not tell you, dear,
which hat I wear.
No, not the nacho hat.
No, not the fish hat.
No, not the one made of straw,
nor the one composed of fig leaves,
it's not the one that smells,
not the one of brightest green,
not the one that attracts pigeons
or the one with the rose attached to the brim.

No, not the tall one I wore as Lincoln that year,
No, not the furry one with the stuffed paws on front.
No, not the swimmer's cap
nor my favorite pillbox,
not the rainproof one
nor the canvas one.
Not the striped one
nor the one with pointy thorns.
Not the black one with the red dot,
not the red one with the black hawk.
Not the turban or the cap,
the beanie or the fedora,
not the yarmulke or the scarf–
my dear, is that even a hat?

Oh yes, I wore it once
just so to make you laugh.

I remember that yes, very fondly.

You give up?

I am not wearing a hat.
I wanted to see how many you could remember.
That is why I love you.

Now meet me at the fountain.
I found a new game for us to play.

CORRECTION

You teach film, too?
So do I.

If by teach you mean
that you
talk during movies.

OVER / UNDER THE CAPE OF GOOD HOPE

When I discovered that
I admired different things
than most of the people
who surrounded me,
I was delighted,
surprised,
and above all,
still very poor.

2012

In time
In our time
In hours time
In four hours' time
In for our time
In for our time out
In a four hour timeout
In a fjord are timeouts

In a fjord, our time is out.

So hold me close,
and pass the crackers.
Because the water level is rising,
and this fjord won't hold forever.

HAROLD THE CONQUEROR

In the time of yore there lived a tiny, tiny man.
He was great in courage, large in wit,
but the puniest in stature, the size of your thumb.
He lived among the rabbits in the grass,
knowing none of his own kind–
for there *were* none of his own kind.

He had shrunk down to his tiny, tiny size
from UV rays deflected off the north pole,
which also wiped out his memory.
Had he remembered everything before the incident,
he would have recalled
that his name was Harold,
that he had a wife,
and that he was absolutely terrified of rabbits.

Lucky for him.

For now, shirtless, he *rides* the great rabbits,
screaming war cries,

spearing rollie pollies for his meals,
his strong, tiny thighs squeezing Thumper's neck,
his hands gripping tight the hair of the hare.

He rides, bare-back, Harold the conqueror!
Hear his shrillish war cry!
Harold! Harold!
Tiny man, rider of the hares,
Ruler of what was once the backyard of his very own house.

Now some guy named Steve lives there,
banging Harold's grief-stricken wife.

HOMER HAD IT SLIGHTLY CORRECT

Look around, you fool.
There is no more *rebellion*.
You and your clay-pot-making friends
will soon be silenced forever.
Your spinning wheels and foot pedals and large ovens
are almost all but wiped from the public's memory.

And once I've seized control of the Senate,
I will command the history guild
to wipe your names from the Book,
and then smash every last one of your
puny, fragile containers
and forevermore will flowers only know the feel of steel,
and soil will know only the cold
and generation upon generation
will place their utensils in cardboard boxes.

Now tell me: where is the one you call the chosen one?

ROAD AWAKENING

If you sit in the middle,
it's not so bad.

NORTH OF THE BORDER BUT SOUTH OF SANITY

When I was a young boy,
I didn't have much time
for shenanigans.
All of the other boys would laugh
and push one another
and throw sticks at each other's eye balls.
They'd come up to me
and ring my doorbell
and ask me to come play
and I'd slam the door in their face
at age eight,
having seen it in *Dallas* one time,
and return to my room
and keep stitching my oven mitts
(that I'd sell out of my backpack)
while listening to discordant music.

How did they not understand
that I, the great
oven mitt stitcher
can not be bothered
with a trifling game of tag?

And somehow,
things have not changed.

THAT'S QUITE ENOUGH OF THAT

Around and around the hero traveled,
ordering a bagel from every shop in town
just seeing if they could get the order right.

Excuse me, dear sir!
This is not a whole wheat
bagel,
as I requested!

Oh, also,
are those men robbing you?

MONEY SPEAKS WITH A STRANGE ACCENT

She made awe-inspiring,
intricate attempts
at having a meaningful life.

Then,
a TV fell on her head.

I FORGOT SO MUCH IT CONFUSES ME

I am indebted to so many people
for this moment.
The list of people to thank
is a thousand feet long.
There is a sharp contrast
in the things that disappoint
and the things that I haven't done–
I can't possibly overcome
every shortcoming I've ever had–
is it hot in here?
I'm so sorry for not being there,
I'm so sorry for not calling you back
It's certainly hot in here–
way too hot for me.
I am surrounded on all sides by expectant eyes
and folded arms
and voices of reproof.
I can't always control everything
and there is too much on my mind
and I never thought there would be an end to this
but now there certainly is and there needs to be more
but I don't have any more.

Where I once considered myself a
meaningful, important waterfall,
I now realize I am merely a large kiddie pool
that some fat kid is peeing in.

A RUN IN WITH MY DISTANT PAST

Damn my insurrections!
They never work
as I would have them work.

I tried an insurrection
at my office–
I passed out pamphlets,
proselytized to my coworkers,
organized meetings,
made picket signs,
bought a megaphone and yelled into it
the most slanderous of opinions.

I roused the masses
to unparalleled passions–
they saw the injustices
the power struggles
the fraud
the cheating
the skimming
the hedging
the casual Fridays not taken seriously.

And through the lines
we would not cross!
We chanted and boycotted
and camped and barked
and we got smelly and stinky
with our bodies odorous yet determined,
for we wanted autonomy!
We wanted brevity!
We wanted more pudding with lunch!

And through the cold winter I felt my power grow.

The people, though, they grew weary,
and some said to give in
was our only hope.
The higher-ups would never budge, they said.
And the days and nights grew thin
and the signs didn't fly so high anymore

and the children cried for mother's milk
and the wind came howling through
and rations were low
and we soon ran aground with deserters of plenty
and found spies in our midst.
(We promptly hung them,
yet this did little
for our lingering spirits.
Though it helped.)

And on a bright day in April
the sun suddenly shone through the wispy clouds
and I felt a power raging inside me
and the people could see it
they could feel it
(some could smell it)
and I rose to the occasion
I stepped up the morale
I re-screamed through the megaphone
the most insidious uprising speeches
the white-collar world had ever heard.
And the people, they came!
the people, they rose!
the people, they shouted!
With one voice, we beckoned for
change!
for
glory!
for
autonomous health coverage!
and something about
IPOs!

And the city got wind of our struggle.
And the news-media-force came through
and put us on the screens
and the home watchers pitied us
and moved for us
clicking their money
for our cause!
And the nation watched
And the higher-ups sweated
as the citizens groped for control.

And soon,
the power was mighty enough
the voice was unified enough
the collaboration was complete.

The higher-ups unsaddled themselves
and gave in more than anyone
could have asked for.

They left their offices empty
and fled to their country homes,
and we entered the building
to rebuild a work-force
fair
balanced
increasingly loyal
organic
fresh
Medicare
vacation benefits
404's
stock options
flexible hours
bigger parking spaces
child care
bowling alleys
tea time
really casual Fridays
naked Fridays, even,
music rooms,
and on-site tailoring..

They of course voted me their leader.
I am President and CEO
of a brand new future.

And as I sit here
at seven o'clock on a Friday
still signing papers,
I think nothing else than–

What the fuck did I do?
I don't want to *work*.

AT THE MUSUEM

This man must have been very angry
this man clearly was against the atom bomb
he was saying fuck you to the whole system
he found an intense spirituality in the abstract
he was in touch with a higher power
he was moved by the violence, the atrocities
he needs only oil and canvas to stand up and protest
he knew exactly what he was doing

Look at the intention!
My eyes deceive me but surely my heart does not.
The strokes are incredible
the color sublime
the choice of balance angelic
it patters at my very soul
it looms over me
its simple beauty.

Oh how I cannot look away!
Oh how it rips me to my very core!
An artist, a true artist!
Tell me: what was his name?

No sir, let *me* tell *you*–
This is not *just* a fire exit map of this floor– it is art!

HANDSOME ANGELS

These are my first breaths
in many a day.
Never again
will I agree
to do lab testing
for that strange man.

Oh my, is that a pretzel man?
I'll have *two*, please.

CRIME, AGHAST, AND WEST COAST LONGING

There is a giant teddy bear
come alive from experiments
evil and sinister
pouncing around Soho
ten stories tall
trying to smash things.

But it can't.

It's just a giant teddy bear
and even though it's big
it's still only filled with stuffing.

It is trying to crush cars
and it's only buffing them.
At first everyone was afraid
and hurried indoors,
until it was clear
that the giant teddy bear
couldn't even bend a street light.
Everyone laughed
and one man allowed himself to be stepped on
and came out uncrushed
only with some cotton
stuck to his shirt.

The teddy bear's grimace
grew
yet it couldn't exact any revenge—
with no hands
it couldn't even pick up the taunting spectators
and moved so slowly
that it couldn't even
knock them down.
So after three hours
of failed rampages
the teddy bear laid down
right in the middle of Broadway
and wouldn't budge.

I am a negotiator.

I have been called in to
convince the teddy bear
to get up
and stop blocking traffic.
I am doing some research
to find out how teddy bears think.
I have never dealt with
anything like this
before.

Yes, Naomi?
Hi, it's Uncle Paul.
Fine, how are you?
Oh, that's so nice.
Your mommy sure must be proud of you.
Listen, Uncle Paul has some questions about
your teddy bear, Howard.
Oh, he's listening, is he?

Could you put him on, please?

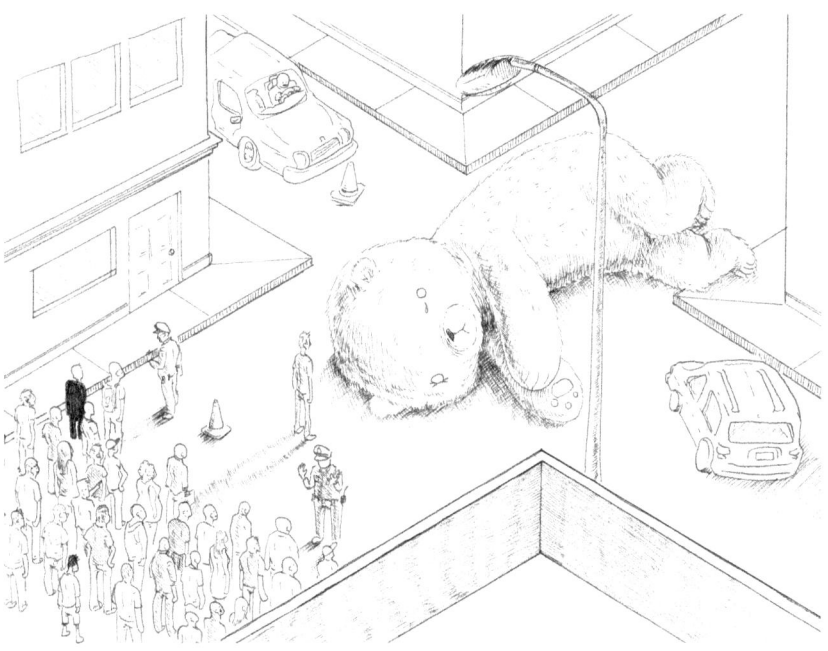

FOR AUSTIN

Here on the Golden Gate bridge
the winds are stronger than I imagined
and I have my arm around a friend I haven't seen in months
(I remember when months seemed like much longer spans of time)
and I'm afraid when the new quick-unit will be years
and we haven't seen each other in two quick-units
oh how I don't want any of this to happen
oh how I don't want three days to end
I will never (perhaps) see this combination again–
the time the bridge the sun the wind the people
the combinations are astronomically rare
and though I am grateful for the back-of-the-mind perspective
I know that it will slip through my calendar even faster–
what does it mean to make it stick?
And why do we want it to?

I'm looking out at a city I don't know very well
wondering what it would be like
to point and know where I'm pointing
without touching a set of goggles or a phone
or some awful fucking combination of both.
What if I had been here instead?
What if by some combination of events and influences
outside my control
I had wanted to be here instead of
way over there?
I am racing backwards now
replaying the events
and trying to delete my experience
and add three quick-units of new ones.
I am negating many good things along with the bad
and losing track of time.

And Austin taps my shoulder
and asks me
where you at?

I laugh
sip my coffee
point down to the sea below
and say look, there's a beach ball.

A PRAYER ON THE PRARIE

It is a fine and fair day, my dear,
You and I gallivanting about in this springtime meadow.
I've packed a light lunch of strawberries and luscious prunes.
Yes, I know how much you like them.
Oh, the grass is fresh cut and trimmed and spreads endlessly!
The Andes in the far background looming over us
like cataclysmic titans hellbent on revenge.
Hold my hand, darling, and frolic forth with me!
We've left all of our cares back at the house
and it will be weeks time before we retreat back
and resume the troublesome lives we've built for ourselves.
No mortgages, bills, work, or children!

Mm?

No, I thought they were staying with *your* mother.

WARM UP PANTS

I was the first one
on the moon.
No matter what that idolator
says.
Just because he went
with NASA,
and had a televised
walk,
he goes down in history.

But no one seems to remember
that in 1937
way before anyone even thought to go,
I ate something weird
and went there in my *mind*.

How does no one remember that?

PRIZE FIGHTING SPELLING BEE CHAMPION

Rotate it to the left, no, too much,
a little back, quite,
you've almost got it,
you're almost there,
you, you, you...
lost it.

You'll never get it back.

We had a moment
and now it's gone, sped away on horseback.
the moment is galloping
top speed,
towards the horizon
ridden by a dirty cowboy
who chews spit tobacco
treats women poorly
and never wonders about the majesty of our moment
that he will eventually
plug with bullets
once they reach camp
and they're far enough away from the sheriff
who is constantly looking in the sky
desperate for a pillar of smoke—
any clue to get our moment back.

He is an honorable sheriff,
one of the good ones,
one of the honest ones,
a man with "character" tattooed on his chest
and, incidentally,
a tiger on his right calf.

The question is:
Who do you want to be?
The cowboy?
The sheriff?
Or you?

Oh, and you can also be the tiger if you wish.
But then you'd always be hungry.

THERE AND BAR

In the brightness of a new morning
oh, I've never been up this early!
The people are beginning to amaze me—
they have neither sunken faces or sallow skin
neither forlorn attitudes nor downtrodden paces
not withered hope nor exasperated dreams
not bitter disappointment or tired agony
they are without the scraping resentment
the desperate futility
the lost passion
the fizzled energy
the knowing of the sadness
all of them are bright and bouncy
and fit as fiddles
and rounded shoulders and calves
right angles on suits
color coordinated
eyes looking forward
looking ahead to the day
knowing exactly where to go and when
slurping down tasty beverages
sprightly in conversation
polite
together
somehow more complete than everyone I know.

These people all went to bed together
and rose up together
and came at the day with the same vigor
that they always do.

I just want to go up to one of them
tap them on the shoulder
and ask one question:
who died
to make you this way?

QUELL QUELL QUELL

Your look
says it all.
I can tell
what you want.
Just come out
and ask me.
I won't be offended.
Why would you hesitate towards potential bliss?
If I am to be the father
to your bodily children,
don't you think it wise
that we should say a few words first?
Get to know each other?
Exchange allergy stories?

Why are you getting on that train?
Don't go!
I have so many family recipes!

FIELDS OF PRIMAL URGES TILLED UNTIL BONE DRY

Snooping around in my sister's den,
I found a list
of things
she doesn't like about me.
I wouldn't have been
so hurt
if it weren't for number five.

I may smell,
I may leave hair in the drain,
I may snore,
I may steal her dolls,
but I do not
love Dad more than her.
Doesn't she know
that all love is equal?

FAME AND HEART

I don't have time
for rumors about
Grandpa.
I'm sure he was a
magnificent lover,
but I'm late for
clay-modeling class.
I am the clay today—
can you not see
that I am covered in it?
I paste this disgusting
mud
all over me
once a week,
and you never take notice.

What do I have to do
to get you to shut up
about Grandpa?

This is no time for laughing,
you elderly hussy.
I will cut off your groceries
so damn fast,
you'll be pushing that panic button
to get the police
to bring you some bread.

THE FUTURE OF ADMIRATION

I once thought
that to grade an essay
was to achieve stability.
Really all that it means is that now
I spend my Sundays
grading essays.

OH CAT

I am often bothered, nay, perturbed,
by a cat that will not sit still for me to pet.
What, do I smell?
What, are you afraid that I will hit you?
What, do my cat ears not look real?

Because I bought them from a man
who swore to me
that you, oh cat, would swoon at the sight of them.
They are sewn from the finest cat fur.
(Imitation of course— no cats harmed for me.)

And my paw gloves?
Are these not acceptable, oh cat?
Why, because they don a rubber bottom?
I think that you are an elitist cat, oh cat,
You only sniff what your refined nose
gives approval to.

Oh cat! Oh cat! Oh cat!

I have a tail now, imported from Burma!
Is that enough for you? No?

Will it *ever* be enough,
Oh cat?

UP AND CLOWN

On top of the needle
beside the fireplace
underneath the rug
before the palimpsest
concerning ninety degree angles
but what about the lawn ornaments?
beyond the ability to climb a large rock
short of time needed to prepare properly
against the inner lining of a loved one's stomach
along the cheering crowd line at the NYC marathon
amid the suspicions of the neighbors' sons and daughters
cradled in the graphs and charts of large, fraudulent corporations
shrouded by comforting yet completely insincere compliments
sidled by the man who swore you were nothing in his grand scheme
swearing that the form meant nothing to you after all
disappointed by the outcome but secretly loving the method
outlandish and true and wanting nothing but feverish redemption
the will to go on and blindly fall forwards into vast uncertainties
thick heavyset powers of the imagination and of wordplay
interactions of verbs and nouns and dreams and worries and environments
the amalgamation of the self and the space and the desire for more
I want to run around with nothing to do and not feel any obligation
I want to sit here and write about it
thickest weather patterns bestowed upon entire regions never imagined
the history of music and the grandeur of knowing it all by heart
and every single note and lyric
they will turn around and talk about you, too
looking in a giant stack of needles for a cliché
turning events over and over in your head before bed
and getting up, forgetting it all, and going to work.
I want to own a boat and sail the California Coast
losing track of which cousin is which
not knowing why he would keep staring, we've never met
avoiding a simple task for the sake of television
condemnation never works
masking motives in words
talousee La Trec–

The kinds of things we say for love
the kinds of things we do for dreams
and echoes of repeated words in this book.

ENCHANTMENT ENTRAPMENT LLYOD

So this one time, I died,
and woke up in heaven.

I walked around for hours in a deserted city
before I finally found a baker
putting out bagels in his display case.
I tried to ask him where God was
but he only spoke French,
and I hadn't paid much attention in class.
No money, I managed to trade one
of my shoes
for a bagel–
I was very hungry.
(I found dying to be an exhaustive experience.)

I rambled the empty streets
looking for God,
and yet he was nowhere to be seen.
The streets were deserted
as if he found out I was coming
and ordered everyone to leave.
I was sad that heaven should be
such a lonely place.
I slackened my pace
and decided not to worry–
that I would find my place
eventually.

Down an alleyway,
I saw a little boy,
haggard and decrepit,
pulled straight from a Dickens novel,
holding a balloon.
He saw me see him
and ran off.

I screamed after him, and broke into a trot
and found that
unlike in movies
a full grown adult can absolutely outrun a child.
Think about it–

their legs are smaller,
and they take smaller strides.
I easily overtook him,
popped his balloon (I was annoyed),
and slapped him (he wouldn't shut up),
and demanded that he tell me
where everyone was.

More importantly,
where was God?
Where the fuck is he, you little brat?
Stop crying, you little shit!
Answer me!

A little light blinked in his eyes
and through tears,
he muttered a feeble and pathetic,

Over my dead body, newbie.

He was surprisingly strong,
it turned out—
he grabbed my hand,
tossed me over his shoulder,
and spit in my ears.
Then he ran away.

I must have blacked out,
because I woke up
tied to a leather chair,
like a dentist's,
and there was a bright light above me.

From the black void beyond
a warm voice, masculine and strong and reassuring,
began to speak.
It told me a long and boring story,
one that I couldn't really follow.
For one, the omnipotent-feeling voice
was terrible at telling stories.
He kept stammering over unimportant details,
kept going back and inserting key elements that,
he assured me,

would pay off later (they never did),
and worst of all,
he kept on forgetting to change people's names
for the sake of the story.
He'd start talking about how shameful Maude felt
when she realized her hand actually *was* in the cookie jar,
and then would quickly correct himself,
and say,
I mean, Maud…lin. Maudlin.
After a few of these instances,
I finally let out a sigh
and rolled my eyes.

For this, a bottle was jammed in my ear,
and I was told to be silent.

The voice finished his story
(at long last)
and asked me
what Maude did.

You mean Maudlin? I asked.

There was a great silence,
and then the cuffs were lifted
off me
the lights turned on,
and all around me,
a coliseum of creatures cheered my name.

The sun appeared,
and God was there,
above me,
a thousand feet high
looking like King Triton.
He smiled, and said I'd passed.

Annoyed, I rubbed my wrists
and asked
so what the *fuck*
happened to the dinosaurs?

WELCOME TO COLLEGE

Place the diamond in the bag,
and step back against the wall!

AN EXPLOSIVE HAND

Top of the morning to you, humming man.
I see that once again you have your morning newspaper
and bright yellow fedora
and are skipping sprightly down the block.
Of course, you're humming, aren't you humming man?
Always in the best of spirits, aren't you, humming man?
What are you humming this time?
Another famous show tune?
A sitcom theme song, perhaps?
Well, I've got news for you, humming man.
I found out about your past.
And you may be fooling the rest of this
naïve little town
with your happy go lucky demeanor
and your *American in Paris* jingles,
but you can't fool me,
and you can't fool history.

So go on your way, humming man.
I've got your number
and be warned:
I've already hidden every copy of *The Hardy Boys*
that the town library had.

GO FIGURE EIGHT

In the event of my death
the lawyers will come knocking
and want to give you something—
do not open the door.

My will has been booby-trapped!

THE FRENCHMAN

You cannot put a price on art.
But this turd is really going to cost you.

PULL ME AWAY FROM THE GULF

I'm looking right at you.

There is a determination in your eyes
a persistence in your demeanor
you have a sharp jaw
the kind that I look for
you have a skinny, athletic face
and walk around pouting about seemingly nothing
because once I start talking to you
you are all smiles
and you let me know that you still
have a lot of life left inside you.

Yet once I get to know you
and your routine
I can see that you are at the end of it
that you've given up
that you're stuck in a rut
that you would only
bring me down further.

So I'm sorry.

No, sir, I'm very sorry.
It looks like
this was not
the rabbit I thought it was.
Good day.

[Ring-a-ding-ding]

THE INTERN

A new kind of bacteria—
the scientists take a closer look
through expensive telescopes.

God damn it, Hal.
Who ordered *tele*scopes?

NOT EVEN CLOSE TO FINISHING

I am not much a fan of limits,
of times to have to be and places to occupy,
yet I am surrounded by barkers of responsibility.

The hippies had some of it right
when they said that life is a flower-pie,
but my father had part of it right, too,
when he told me to take some business classes.
As always, I am somewhere in the
glorious middle,
one foot plunged deep in a giant, warm flower pie,
the other foot exacting figures on a foot-calculator.

My biggest conundrum
is that both do good things for my feet.
On the one foot,
the petals are gooey and wrap themselves
between my toes,
and people seem to really like my flower-pie foot.

On the other foot,
I am being so damn
productive.
You should see how adeptly my pinky toe
clickity-clacks the square root button.
It is a thing
that even my flower pie brethren
might appreciate.

I would hope that it would be as simple
as choosing between which foot to
take out and which one to step towards,
but life is never Column A and Column B
it's column 1, 2, apple, tiger, fierce, could, *ayuda*–

And my hands are occupied as well–
my left hand is stirring a bowl of grits,
adding flax seeds, raisins, almonds, and soy milk,
my right hand is cupping a puppy
trying to keep it happy and fed
my lower left hand is playing guitar

my lower right hand is trying to learn Mandarin
my upper left hand is wearing beads and won't shut up about Louisiana,
my upper right hand is crossing its fingers and hoping for nothing in particular
my center hand is tickling some girl
my back hand is playing tennis
my diagonal hand is trying to read its own future.

Lord only knows
what the fuck my head is doing.

THE LUSCIOUS BOBBY DARIN

The bobbing of heads on the dancing floor
reminds me of sea anemones
on my trip to Hawaii.
The only difference
between these teens
and those creatures of the deep
is their diet.
They are alike
in every other way.

What is this song?
I've never heard it before.
Bah, I probably shouldn't
chaperone these things
anymore.

I'm feeling
old
and
hallucinogenic.

NOSTRADAMUS

There are new things on the horizon
and they are shaped like blenders—
But why do I need *two* blenders?

YOU SEEM LIKE A NICE OLD LADY

I'm stuck here for a certain amount of time
I have no idea how long.
It's one of those times in your life
When you're in between one thing and another
and you're not ready to stay
and not ready to go.
I am at odds with so many things
I am at the brink of many decisions
I am at a point of teetering hollows
I can see for miles in many directions
I am consistently torn one way and then another.

Oh did I mention that
I'm handcuffed to a parking meter?

PLACE YOUR EVERLASTING TRUST IN EXPIRED CREDENCE

Everything is internal, friends.
I do not need the external
for my art.

What use is a sunset?
What inspiration comes from a
passing subway car?
I need not open my door
to travel the world.
I put pen to paper
and unfold the subversive impressions of prescient memory.

What, what is that you say?
A bus?
Where a bus?

No, I need not look up
to see a bus bearing down on me.
thank you very

LOOK BACK ON YOUR TURBULENT YOUTH

I cannot put my finger on why,
but for some reason,
I cannot dance.
It may have something to do with the fact
that I am a stool
and this is merely
personification.
Fine, I get that.

But if I can speak,
why can I not also dance?

Also, why do I have a finger?

THE LIVID CONCLUSION

The box rattled and shook
back and forth
in the middle of the empty room.
They had almost completely moved out
and had left this shaking, rattling, cardboard box
right in the middle of the empty room.
I wanted to throw it on the street
and let the garbage man deal with it
yet I didn't want to touch it.
I sat next to the box for hours
thinking of what to do
and the shaking and the rattling
lulled me to sleep
and I woke up hours later
covered in snakes.

Oh, you guys!
You jokesters!

DOUBTFUL

I'm very sorry, I can no longer
approve this message.

THE TORNADO HAS OUR CHILD'S NOSE

It is the early afternoon
and I have already gone for a run
studied hieroglyphics
called my mother
learned a new song on piano
worked an eight hour shift
painted a nude
nuded a painting
pianoed a new song on learning
quilled a declaration or two
bred a few new breeds
combined elements no one has heard of
scrambled some eggs
organized my room
clefted apart siamese twins,
experimented with the opposite sex
discovered a new way to kiss
(it's with the back of the neck)
guessed a large man's weight exactly
skipped for ten straight blocks
drew from my experience to learn a thing absolutely
resoluted to never do two things again
disconnected from the grid
reverted to a few old habits
tapped on an old wooden door
asked a few questions of the old man on the mountain
demanded answers from a strange baby
realized who it was I didn't like anymore
snorted a line of kiwi seeds
bicycled to Portland and back
planted a new tree (the one of knowledge)
(I found the tree of knowledge yesterday
and stole two seeds)
designed an entire city
threw a baseball into the clouds
drank a pint of whiskey with a swarthy Frenchman,
lost my house in a game of poker
and then won it back in a game of canasta
shaved off my beard
shaved off ice and flavored it and sold it to some dumb kid,

balanced on my head on Astor Place cube
read the important parts of a boring book series,
made sense of women
figured out what "in the bag" meant
took a shower under the stars
paddled from Mauna Loa to the Big Island
bobbled a ball in record-setting weather conditions
played the guitar for a million screaming fans
who all swore their lives had changed afterwards
made fun of an untouchable comedian
pushed aside the President at a rally
gave the finger to the camera
ran through a lilly field and had a tickle fight with a squirrel
laughed until I saw spots
took apart an old engine and reworked it
fitted myself for a suit
wired a car to spy on an enemy of mine
reworked my resume
dead ended my life
sucked up to the right people
compiled a list of applicable verbs
struck down the gods with their own lighting bolt
wrapped myself in giant swaddling clothes
hammered together a rather nice bird house
modeled a clay bust of Grover Cleveland

disgusted myself away from all business
graded a few papers
smoked a few joints
wrote a few poems
read some Henry Miller
connected us back again
nodded my head to some discordant beats
remembered the good times
calculated my monthly expenses
fitted some new jeans
looped the thread in the mix
castrated my neighbor's dog
rolled my eyes at a few bystanders

and then found you,
and began to rest.

THE BRIGHT SIDE OF LIFE

A few of them have walked by me
and not asked about what I am writing.
How am I supposed to be
that mysterious artful stranger turned love interest
if no one will stop to talk to me?

It must be my smell.

LEGEND

It is the day of days–
the sun is in perfect alignment
with Saturn
and so the winds
are very cool and heavy today.

So rise up, youth!
Steal the sword of entitlement
from under Uncle Harry's work bench!
He keeps it there
because he knows
it's the last place you'll look.

Once you've attained the sword of entitlement,
thrust it upwards towards the heavens,
and if you mutter the right incantations,
a lightning bolt will come through both of the planets
carrying with it the core elements of
both
those celestial bodies,
and like a surging outlet,
will jolt the sword
with more entitlement
than you've ever dreamed.

So use it wisely.
No wait–

Don't!

THE RECKONING

Look around,
but not too much.
This is familiar to you, I know,
but officially you've never been enrolled here.
And if the chancellor ever gets wind
that I used to bring you here as a child,
then it's both our asses.

Now shh, grab a pencil,
and stay close.

CLOSE YOUR EYES AND I'LL BRING YOU A CROISSANT

I'm finding it hard to concentrate
to hold this pen in its proper place
I want to wish that for hours we could
be together,
but muscles are fickle maidens
and they hardly ever do
exactly as they please.
I find that if I ease up
and relax
and stop trying so hard
stop gripping so tight
that my muscles easier obey me.

I have a goal in mind that we will dance all day
The visions of my future are always eluding me–
they're never what I really wanted,
and yet I get up again and do it all over.

A friend of mine in college once told me
that there is no such thing as repetition,
yet I'll try and try again and bare my forehead onto this desk
for on days like today
I am truly free.

B YOURSELF

Nicolai Gogol's work is being underlined right now
by some asshole
in some public place
to make you feel stupid.

The title is showing outward –
He knows what he's doing.
Or does he?
I've always wondered.
Is he the perpetrator?
Or is he a witless victim,
unaware of social mores and customs,
or are there no customs for this?
Am I making it all up?
Is no one else
seeing this like I am?
Just put the book lower.
That's how I would do it.

Ah! That bright light
through the train's window!
It's so damn blinding!

I can still see the title of the book,
I am disappointed to find out.

Maybe I should shut up
and just start reading Gogol.
It would be a first on two fronts.

A BUM WITH A CART

There are moments buzzing around us
like flies.
Some people live in the moment,
looking at each fly in wonder.
Yet some are more like me,
quickly running for the flyswatter.

A FUCKED UP THIRD GRADER

When there's nothing left to do
at the end of time,
when the clouds have finally lifted,
and the sky has split open,
and the earth has spilled molten lava all over its cities,
and disease has ravaged the populations,
and war war war,
and you are left standing on a mountain
watching the sea level rise
because of the ice caps melting,
and it's only a matter of minutes
until you are swallowed whole
and sharks rip apart your limbs...

Will you *then* be my valentine?

THE CRIMEAN WAR

I want to return to a time when
Our dignity reigned supreme.

When images held no stronghold,
when thought prevailed
when people actually read.
I want to go back in time
when arguments were well thought out,
when history was remembered
when ancient wars were known–
when you *knew* a guy.

Things were so simple.
I want to go there
and show them the internet.

Look at all the boobs! I'll say.

LATE NIGHT RAIN RUN

The time we went running in the rain
was perhaps my favorite memory of us.
Do you remember that?
You were wearing those bright blue sweatpants
and those glasses with the straps to protect them from falling off
and that jacket with the tiger with sunglasses on the lapels
and those socks with the individual toes
and that underwear with the president's face on the ass—

We met in the underpass of the bridge
and knew that it was bad idea
and held hands and counted three
and leapt out in the cold pour
and were only out for a few minutes before we realized
how silly it was to try to run
for it was coming down so heavy and we couldn't see
and they had turned off the lights in the park
and we stumbled around and sloshed through the grass
and sank our feet in deep puddles
and then eventually stopped and found a bench
and I kissed you better than I ever have
and it was probably my best kiss ever
and then you started laughing
and I said why are you laughing
and you said because I'm breaking up with you.

Who the hell breaks up with someone
right in the middle of a rain run?

FUNCTION OF ZERO

The time will come
when *you* will be changing
my diaper.
So stop crying,
or I will remember this
and cry harder.

PROVING TRUE THE SUSPICION OF NIGHTLY DRILLING

The wallpaper is thick with enmity
or is it just thick?
I'm running my hands all over it
and there seems to be
something bumpy underneath.

Someone is banging on the door,
wanting to use the bathroom as well.
I twaddle my fingers over it one more time,
mystified,
and open the door.

I brush my way past the newcomer,
and am back among the social elite,
the packed loft
the fluorescent-lit bar
with the handsome, taut
bartender
who gave me smarmy looks
when I asked for a
beer and cranberry juice
and he handed them to me
separately and I said,
no, dolt!
Mix them!

I do not want another drink.

I amble through the crowds
and their conversations
sting my ears
with their obsessions with taxes,
trigonometry,
children,
ergonomics,
pacifiers,
and titillating romance novels.

I cannot but help but scoff at every single one of them.

I am the guest of honor!

How does no one see that
my name
my face
is sloppily pasted all over the poster
near the entryway?
How is no one stopping me
and asking me
what it is like to be me?
All of their eyes are turned
and none of them fix upon me,
even though it is I
who have discovered
the recipe for
the world's most delicious
rugelach.

Before me, the world
had never known such rugelach!
What bland taste buds we seemed to love
before I unveiled my creation!
How ungrateful these socialites are!
Chatting and drinking and flirting and dancing
taking no notice of me
and how great
I really am.

I'm shoving my hands in my pockets
and pushing my way through–
they recoil at how rude I am
but still they take no notice.
They declare,
they've never,
they can't believe,
and I with my head down
finally make my way
to the dessert table.

Full.

Untouched.

Pristine.

Rugelach.

Not one had been taken.
Piles of it on silver platters
in the center of the room—
perhaps one or two have been sampled,
but hundreds remained.

This was my spark.

Like Jesus at the Temple,
I overturned the tables
onto the dance floor.
All of my rugelach,
the most delicious rugelach
the world has ever known,
crushed under the feet of simians.

I had an improvised speech
swelling up inside me
and I was ready to chastise
these ticks
for wasting what could have been
the most delightful experience
their tongues have ever had.
I had a harangue
that none would have believed.

Yet even with the noise of
three upturned tables
and hundreds
maybe thousands
of pieces of rugelash
strewn all over the floor
and under their feet,
no one turned.
No one noticed.
No one
stopped dancing.

I made my way to the roof.
I leaned on the metal railing
and took in the New York City sky.

All was lost,
all was hopeless.
I had spent eleven years of my life
in my basement kitchen
perfecting that rugelach.
All my efforts
were a drop in the bucket
of the world's lives.
Apparently
no one cares about
rugelach
as they did in the eighties.

Smoking my rugelach flavored cigarrete
(an invention I would have revealed
as a bang
if they had cared to notice me)
I shook my head.

Then she came.

I heard the door open behind me
and a woman came through.
Her beauty
made all pastries
pale
in comparison.

She asked if she could lean with me
and I assented.
She asked if she could smoke
and I assented.

I held her in my arms
and she wheezed a sigh of gratitude
and told me
she loved my rugleach,
and had been looking
all over for me.

I'm right here,
I said.

WHAT IS THAT ON THE WING?

Why oh why did the little birdie fly
and what is that on the wing?
so close from the nest it's flapping
his little undeveloped bones
and what is that on the wing?
he is trying so hard not to look back
and the wind is such a burden
and the trees need maneuvering around
and what is that on the wing?
down through the valley
over the river
under the mistletoe—
what the hell is that on the wing?
the little birdie has gone so far
and tested the limits of his first flight
and the legend of girl-bird island is oh so close
it's right there, a hundred yards ahead
the place his father warned him about
the siren-like Atlantis
and he begins to salivate all over his beak
just picturing the girl-birds in their nests
and what is that on the wing?
he can practically hear them now
and his private feathers are ruffling themselves
and— seriously, what is that on the wing?

It's me! Me, you foolish bird, it's *me* on your wing!
You didn't notice a full-grown man in a recliner
enjoying a free ride to bird-girl island?

And it's bird-*girl* island, not girl-*bird*!
Those sirens are mostly human!
You wouldn't know what to do with a feathered vagina,
but I sort of do!

NEW YORK IN THE SKY

After-hours in the cafe:
All the workers stand on stilts
and throw mugs at each other!

INTERNATIONAL SABOTAGE RELIEF PARTY

A crying baby panther
A loose-lipped captain and his crew
A cackling nemesis spinning a top.
Where have we ended up
that we cannot be all of these?

Why must I sweat like a man
and not slip like a salamander?
Why do I not have plates on my back
like a triceratops?
Or a plate spinner?

I spin around and around
muttering my questions aloud
getting dizzy
throwing up
covering my mouth with both hands
unable to keep it all in
it's spewing through my fingers now
trickling down my arms
and I'm still spinning
muttering my plate questions
letting my mind go.

How do you sleep at night, answer man?
Answer me that, answer man
you think you have them all
you claim that you never spin and throw up
but I can see the stains on your sleeves
and crusted remnants on the corner of your mouth.

When you're alone at night in your palace,
and there's nothing more on the radio,
And the quiet sets in,
don't tell me you don't wonder why
you're not a tidy CEO with down syndrome.

You don't know the answer, answer man,
so admit it: you spin and throw up like the rest of us.

Admit it!

IN THE SPRING I KNEW THAT I LOVED YOU

Foresight is an afterthought,
a before-thought is premonition,
memory is useless,
baseball is boring.

GROWING ON THE WINDOWSILL

I am sitting on top of a mountain
looking out at every city below
and even from here
I can tell the voting districts are divided unfairly.
Where can we possibly
live objectively?

HEMINGWAY SPEAKING FRENCH

I had a dream last night
that today was going to be a beautiful day,
and indeed it has become
exactly that.

Except for
all these damned Howitzers
rumbling through the streets.

Those were
quite the surprise.

WAKING GOODNESS

I have heard this song already.
Play a different one!
Yeah, that's good.
That's a good beat there.

Now *this* is a funeral!

PROBABLY A TRIFLING QUERY

I am lying on my side
I am lying about what really happened that night.

I am an apathetic smile,
A robust lover,
a disguised onlooker,
sunglasses and a trench coat.

They tell the crowd to move on,
nothing to see here,
please disperse folks.

But we are a curious bunch
we want answers
and you cannot dispel an idea.

They want to see what's underneath
the large blanket in the street
that the newspapers are taking pictures of.

I, however, know what's inside.
The police can't hold back
the advancing crowd,
they are pushing and inching
mumbling now speaking
amassing one body
pressing forward
feet skidding, palms outstretched.
They are making the demands
They raise their fists then their brows
They are shouting over heads
And now the blanket in the street is under them
And someone throws it back
to reveal it all.

It is an impossible light
That winking, twirling mist
that spins us asunder.

And now I'm smiling
Because they all fell for it.

OH, THE TANNINS!

My back aches and my head is clear.
Oh, god, how my head has never been more clear!
There are so many thinking citizens
in this world,
and they are all pushing one another—
brave, complicated minds
proving to one another that we're worthy,
and I don't doubt that we are,
what I do doubt,
my lonely companions,
is whether or not
I can tolerate
An unripe cantaloupe.

Have you ever had an unripe cantaloupe?
It makes you want to lazily kill yourself.

ARE YOU SAD? THEN SCREW YOU, MAN

If it were only as easy as putting the pieces together,
but I have to worry about progression,
about ascension
about the feelings along the way
of part to a whole
of examples of unity in history.

I got an A in organizational management,
but who would have thought
that a circus
would be so much work?

THURSDAY

"I missed the mark
when I married you."
How the hell
did you think I would take that?

THIS IS THE FUTURE

Oh what a convention it is
to do the thing that lies in front of you!
Such expectation you fulfill,
The thousands upon trillions of pairs of eyes
that watch in stillness
waiting for your fist to jump through a hoop
and your arm to follow
then your head and body and
pointed feet,
landing in a prepared body of water
and expecting so little of a splash.
Their scoreboards are waiting.

(And even this you expect me to finish soundly,
to tidy up with
all of these things I can feel in my head
inbred by years of conditioning
and aren't we at least
a little sick and tired
of all the things we think we want to see?)

So you emerge from a pile of sand,
spit fire at the scoreboards,
burn the synagogue to the ground,
and form a posse
with the unwilling survivors.

AAAAAA

It's only addicting
if you let it be.
I have yet to find out
if I can resist the laurels of taste
that adorn my head
and drip into my mouth–
for it tastes sweet,
like cigarette juice and cocaine gas.

LOVE ADVICE

Is it ever too soon to tell someone you love them?
Yes.
Of course it is.
What if you had just met this person?

They say, Hi, I'm Karen,
I'm your new secretary.
And you say, Hi Karen, I'm Bill,
your new boss.
Ha ha, I think I'm in love with you.

Hi Bill, I'm your cell mate, Gunther.

I know, I know.
It is certainly not fair, I agree.
But what do you expect, Bill?
Besides, she's way out of your league.

Aim lower,
and keep your mouth shut.

AN EXCUSE FOR TARDINESS

I don't want to end up like you –
all provided for,
happy,
fulfilled,
child-bearing,
accurately vocabularied,
pool-owning,
hot chocolate drinking,
instrument playing,
independent.

I want to end up just like me now
and die today,
because tomorrow I was going to start turning myself
into someone
more like you.

BRAD

The voice is now speaking
in strange and various tones.

I hear that voice, do you hear it?
It's shaking my lobes
echoing in my mind-cave
reverberating on the insides of my scalp.

Excuse me, miss– can you hear it?
Dear sir, do you hear the voice?
Can anyone hear what I can?
I run out into the street,
Stop, car! I say with palm outstretched.
Get out, this is police business.
I throw the pregnant woman to the ground,
and put the pedal to the metal.

I'm screaming and careening down the freeway.
Honk, honk!
Can you hear the voice?
Honk, honk!
Can you hear it?

I'm heading toward the cliff now,
the road is ending.
I crash through the signs that read
Road Rlosed
The dust kicks up and I am reeling.
I can still hear the voice.

I call into a radio show
They say
Congratulations, you're our fifteenth
caller!
You get a free hat and an entry in
our grand sweepstakes and–

Shut up! I say frantically.
Can you hear the voice? I ask.

He says, go to a commercial,

This guy's a nut.
No wait, I say.
Listen to this, I say.

And as my car is sailing through the air,
nose down,
A Thelma without my Louise,
I hear the voice one last time,
And it's saying hello to its mother,
because it can't believe it's on the radio.

MORE THAN WE BARE TO OUR CHILDREN'S PETS

Just in time to
slide through the doors
unnoticed.
No one looks up
to see what amazing
cans of peaches
I am balancing
on my shoulder blades.

The subway car is packed tight
and the people—
busy-bodied, forlorn, sleeping, perhaps—
couldn't be woken from
their various slumbers
if I shouted rape-fire-terrorist.

So my peaches do not impress?
My years of balance training
from all the women in Cairo
were all in vain?
What about the slinky
sitting atop my head?
It stands like a coil-stack,
unhinged,
unfulfilling the destiny of its name
with my perfect posture.

No?

What, then, of the marbles in my eyes?

Two of them in each socket,
both the size of pool balls –
wait, they are pool balls!
My furrowed Italian brows
can hold two pool balls each!
I am almost a walking
symbol of the Olympics!

Will no one take notice?
Fine then.

I resort to the most extreme measures.

I begin to recite
The Federalist Papers
from memory
Backwards
in Greek
doing a headstand.

Still no one?

Fine. My penis will then
don a wig
and be my sideshow clown.

Sleepers, all of them still.
New York is a hard place
for us attention whores.

So we keep trying.

BEGINNING

Is it too much to fancy, to ask, to plea,
to be able to rise high above the clouds
drop food on all the nations that need it
and change the weather for the better?

Is that really
too much to ask?

CANDY

If you tell me that
you'd like to start
A Brand New Religion,
you'd better be prepared
to put in the work.

Because I tithe to no lazy.

PILES AND PILES OF HARD WORK, LUCK, AND COLD HARD CASH

If there were a way
to measure how much laughter weighed
you'd think that hyenas
would have the lion's share.

Look again—
tipping the scales
high above all the competition
are top-level movie executives.

FASHION

My waistline
once had ten servants.

A THOUGHTFUL SECOND ADDRESS

It's been a long time coming—
you've thought that I wouldn't ever find you, I'm sure.
But the picture on the milk carton
matches you exactly.
I'm bringing you home
and getting the reward.

What do you mean
you've never been kidnapped?

HEMINGWAY, PART II

Don't quit while you're ahead, you moron.

CAN YOU FEEL THAT? IT'S SPRINGTIME!

I have a luminous secret
hidden away in
the recesses of my yearbook.
It was my junior year edition,
and on page two hundred,
directly between the glee club profile
and the society for the betterment of
rapturous animals,
lay a two page full spread
of my grandmother
fully nude
laying on a deck
sometime in the 1950's.
I found the picture in a drawer
broke into the yearbook office
and scanned it in
one day before it went to the printer.

My secret is not that I did it.

My secret is that
I also stole twenty dollars out of her purse, weekly,
for most of the time that she was living with us.

Now that she's dead and gone
I open the yearbook every week
and staple a twenty dollar bill
to the legs,
supple as they are,
of my passed grandmother.
There must be seventy-five bills
stapled to the page.

One day,
when I've stapled enough to her,
I'm going to buy her
the coffin she always wanted
instead of that cardboard one
that I settled on last year.

That is my other secret.

BURN THE REASONS AND THE CANDIES

Is it hot up here,
up on the mountain?
My feeling has numbed,
and it has taken away
all of my nerve endings.
It could be very cold,
it could be very hot,
but I'm going to guess
and say that it is very hot.
Yet you are wearing full mountain climbing gear.
And you are wrapping me in a blanket.
And you are rubbing my chest.
And now you are pouring steaming liquid on my face.
And you are crying
And telling me not to go towards the light
And are rocking back and forth.

I'm still going to guess
that it is very hot up here.

Oh my, is the view not
incredibly beautiful from up here?

Wait—
where are you going?

GRIMACE AND GRIT

I don't think we should get too close, baby.
In my profession,
I am constantly
looking over my shoulder.

I love you, too,
but this could put you in danger,
and the last thing I want
is to put you in harm's way.

All right.

I'll tell you.

For many years now, I've been working as
an undercover plumber.

That's right.

I sneak into people's houses,
dressed as the pool boy,
the dog groomer,
the refrigerator repair man,
and once I've gained their trust,
and they leave me to my own devices,
I secretly unclog their pipes.

No, literally.
I tighten up screws to fix leaks.
I make it so the faucet
don't drip no more.
I make the hot water
come out much faster.

No, no one pays me.
I don't bill people for my services.

Because, baby, plumbing is a
higher calling, see.
The act itself is the reward.

But you never know who I'm gonna piss off,
people who liked their faucets drippy, maybe,
who count on the sink backing up a little
and like their dirty, cloggy, filthy lives.
You never know, baby.
They could be after me.

Oh, and yeah, could you spot me a twenty?
I'll pay ya back.

TO DRESS A SONGBIRD (IN SWADDLING CLOTHES)

"Let the record state,
ladies and gentleman of the court,
that the witness has indicated
that he is of sound mind,
temperate judgment,
and balanced psyche.

Look upon him now,
balancing that orange on his nose,
wearing only his trousers,
and singing expired show tunes.

Does he look of sound mind
to you?"

This is what the hot-shot attorney
said
right before he realized
that the jury
was made up of
twelve trouser-wearing
show tunes-singing
seals,
all of them balancing oranges on their nose.

Except for one,
who balanced an apple.

That's my seal, he said to himself,
reforming his strategy.

He plucked an apple from his briefcase.
He was, after all, an excellent attorney.

SEX

How do you know when it's time
for a break?

A LIKELY STORY

I'm running naked through the forest
headlong and steadfast.
My bare feet are crinkling on the leaves
and I'm darting through the trees.
It's cool and foggy and just after dawn
and I'm panting but I can't stop.

I finally stop, close my eyes, breathe deep,
and the cool, New England fall
envelops me
and hundreds of years of human history
wisp through my lungs
and I can feel the pilgrims
making dinner on Plymouth rock
inside my chest cavity.
The Indians are friendly
and eating corn on the cob
and sitting on my capillaries
and getting massages by my expanding and contracting
for I am heaving quite heavily.

I reach a road and step into the clearing
the cars that pass honk their horns
and I give them a thumbs up and smile,
for they are my potential brethren.

I sit on the asphalt
cross legged–
is it already sundown?
I smile to myself and shake my head,
for I know
thyme is a human construct.
I pity those who do not know it.

I let the night come.

The crickets chirp and the wolves howl
and I walk up the road to find shelter
for there will be much more running tomorrow
and I need my rest.

I find a lovely pile of leaves
just on the other side of an embankment.
I am thankful that they are mostly dry
and I crawl headfirst into them
and oh they are so deep!
Easily three or four feet above me,
this will surely be adequate bedding for the night.

I curl up into the womb-ball,
and let the weight of leaves fall upon me.
My breath is warm on those reflective filters,
and I think about how hidden I am
from all the everything
and yet how exposed I am
to the essence of all things.

The kinds of things we believe
The devotion we give to silliest of institutions!
How we are not free
How we are bound
How we are enslaved
The time that creeps by
under our very noses
while we are smelling ready-made pasta.
There are too many facets to all this
to really take in
there are too many countdowns
and fences,
and I wish to liberate the earth
and all its inhabitants
the cats and grass included
from all that we believe that we believe.

The time passes slowly
just as I like it
and as toss and turn
and try to fall asleep
I cannot help but wonder
about
how worried sick
my wife and kids must be.

THE END OF PAGES, TIME, THOUGHT, AND PLAY-TIME

What happened to common decency?

It seems like only yesterday
that gentlemen held doors open
for lovely ladies,
and strangers gave up their seats
in the park,
and people tipped their hats at one another,
that is, of course,
if they were wearing hats.

And they were!
Those were the hat-wearing days
if I've ever heard them.
Days when not a head was uncovered
nor a brow unfurnished.

Our time is running short,
dear friends.
When will a day come when you can no longer
wear a hat?
or say hello?

It comes like a hat in the night,
dear friends,
and it will cover your heads with
forgetfulness
of the time when it was once possible
to be a darling human being.

Darling, I say!

MANIFEST DESTINY

It's iced tea,
you foreigner.

GOD BLESS THE TURNING OF THE TIDE

Listen:
You never said anything to me
about your cousin
sleeping on our couch.
This is a problem
not for me, of course,
but for your cousin,
who now will be subject
to my various, non-sexual advances.

Tell me,
is she privy to knowledge of
Ancient Greece?

GOOD PEOPLE AND BETTER PETS

Yes, that's your grandfather
in that sailor's cap.
No, two to the right.
Yes, the one with the funny face.
Hard to believe he was ever that young,
isn't it?
This photo was taken a long time ago,
before he and your grandmother
ever banged.

Oh, my God, I'm sorry Joel.
I'm still learning
how to be
a good father.

LA

Everyone in this town
is trying to do the same thing.
But not me.
I'm trying to be
an actor.

BEE IS THE ONE, ISN'T IT?

A little child,
perhaps only five or six,
walks down a dark alley.
From this vantage point,
it is difficult to tell whether
it is he or
it is she
but in either case
the little child is in tattered rags
as if from a *Les Miserables* dress rehearsal.

The little child is dragging behind
a cello
a giant cello
in better condition than most.

The child comes into the
yellow light of main street
pauses
and stands the cello upright.

Ah, it's a she.

She closes her eyes
and places a bow between her toes
and plays a beautiful
soft
somber
deep rolling

bellowing
echoing
maddening
rippling
affecting
sonnet
Her fingers are nimble
her toes are surprisingly
grippy.

And as she plays,
she slowly
begins to ascend into the sky
and her eyes are still closed
and she's still playing
but she's ascending higher and higher now
and you crane your neck and
put your hand up to block the yellow light
to see where she has gone
and for maybe a minute
you can see her outline against the full moon
before she's too small
she's still rising
and you're standing where she was
hands in your pockets
your shoes ruffle the gravel
and your jacket is pretty nice.

You're wondering about what to
do next.

When from the sky
what should fall
but the bow.
Perhaps her toes weren't so grippy.

And now the bow is on your mantle
above the fireplace
and when guests ask you,
oh, what is that?

You don't really know what to say.

A STRANGE SOUND

What on earth could you possibly be afraid of?
Change?
Why, that's absurd.
You set out in the first place
with mounds of change in mind
and now that the possibility for change
is here
really here, staring back at you
with its almond blue eyes
you're going to cower and hide
under the guise that things are
usually this way?
Too many people are afraid to really grab at it
and will say things must be this way,
because this is how I've done it before.

So yeah, I know you're tired.
Pick up that flute
march down those halls
and give those cool kids
something to really make fun of you *for*.

TRUE HARVEST

Flickering lights
in an abandoned basement—
When did you do all of this?
There must be
hundreds
of paintings down here.
And they're
all
of me.
No, I'm not creeped out.
In fact, I'm rather impressed.

What's the rubber band for?

FROM PRUSSIA, SIN AMOR

The bounce and step
of a rhythm from a song
sails through the air
with a light, fluttery precision.

I am sitting by an open window
waiting for the wind
to cool my brow.
The trees in the distance sway.
I can see the wind coming,
closer it approaches –
I just may be the first
person
to touch this particular wind.
I am waiting beautifully for it,
and this moment
is everything to me.

Ding!

Shit, my pop tarts are ready.

MY LIFE– (AN HONEST TITLE, FOR ONCE)

I am standing on a stage
I am writing on a page
I am working for minimum wage.

RIGHT THERE, THAT'S PROOF

Try to keep in mind the fact
that penmanship
is on par of importance
with hygiene.

That's why I brush my teeth
with very neat pens
and write my resumes
on bars of deodorant.

DON'T LOOK TOO MUCH AHEAD

Renegade this:
If you're such an icon of rebellion,
what are you doing
with an icon of fashion?
Do you sense a contradiction?
I sense something fishy
in the background
and it might be
something other
than money.

Oh Lord.
Do you actually love each other?
My mistake.
I'm just jealous
on, you know,
a macro-scale.

My apartment is cold
this time of year.

AND THEN HE DIED

It is occupied, sir.
I will be out
presently.
Or rather,
future-ly!

GRAPH THIS

There was once a time
when it was enough
to simply have potential.

Those days
are long gone.

YELLOW BRICK ROAD

Be careful, my young student.
You are not ready for the ways of the world.
To venture without proper training
will only lead you to death.

And be careful, my old teacher,
you are not ready for the totally awesome things
that I'm going to do.
You are pruning and dying
and have no clue
what the bump and grind is.

Be careful, you two.
I am God your father
Your creator
and I'm here to tell you
that no matter what you do,
you're both dead.

So calm down.

SUGAR SWEET MOUNTAIN MAN

I deal in underwear.

EXAMPLE

A curious thing, Disappointment—
it looms in the background
of Hope.

That's why I hire
secret assassins
to slit Disappointment's throat
before it tries to steal the spotlight away from Hope.

I just wish the assassins wouldn't charge so much.

THE ESSENCE OF EXCLUSIVITY

Have you bathed in the rich splendors
of the Sea of Honey?
It's not just a name—
it is a literal sea
of real, bee-manufactured honey.

And oh, is it exclusive!
Some summers, Beatrice and I
take the kids out there
and jump on the giant floater-bounce
and launch each other backwards
hundreds
thousands of feet in the air
and in those floaty-golden moments
my family and I
are in resplendent bliss.

I hang in the air
twisting and turning
looking out across the golden sea
that stretches for miles in each direction
the shores lined with birch trees
gives me solace,
rest,
and a new idea
for my next composition.

I could close my eyes
and still be able to see
that it is everywhere
and that life is art,
and as I reach the apex
a bit sooner than my wife and the kids
and I pass them on my way down
free-falling toward nectar oblivion
the aroma is swilling around me

wafting through my nose
and the magnified clarity of the Honey Sea
rushing towards me.

Everything becomes clear then
Everything is stripped away and pure
Because now I have a new appreciation for the square
for the helix
for DNA
for the rounded corners and simple beauty of a cabin in the woods
and I want to follow my heart
and be someone else that I am
and go out and isolate myself from the bullshit
and not care about what anyone else says about me,
and never worry about profits or margins
or who you know
or where you go

and I turn upwards and see my kids flailing
and my wife smiling
and I'm reminded of a song I heard once
about a boy with a wet dream
or something about satisfaction
I think it was the stones
and I put my hands behind my head
and cross my legs
and close my eyes
and wait for the impact
the beautiful thud
and over the wind
I can hear my kids screaming with joy
saying
Daddy Daddy look I'm a squirrel
and the high-pitched cackle of my lovely wife
(where did I ever find such a woman?)
and know that I love what I am
and who I am
because life is too short
for bad beer.

We thud
we are ensconced
we are stuck thirty feet below
and we are never heard from again
in the Sea of Honey.

TEXT, TIME, AND DEATH

Oh how much work there is to do
to keep up with and maintain.
The fires keep coming
and we the mighty firemen
scurry about and do our duty.

House 39!
On your feet!
The old mill's a-blazing!

We have a million miles to cover
before we'll even see the smoke.
So we'll take the rocket
and hopefully make up some time in the air.

What was it about the speed of light they said?
That it will tear your cheeks apart
revealing your bones
that will also be torn away?

I am at the speed of light,
and the only thing I'm going through
is that I have to pee
and the galaxy is devoid
of urinals.

RETRIBUTION FACTORY

Oh yeah?
Well if I'm so much better off without you,
then what am I doing
sitting in a bathtub full of oatmeal
trying to play the ukelele?

You know how much I hate this.

TULIP TULAY TODAY

Can you feel the change in the air?
The rising sun and the swooning wind?
Do the bird songs reach your ears?
How often does the thistle
of the trees
grab your attention?
How long have you
stared
in the passing, waning
lights of the descending moon?
How much does
the trickle of a gleaming stream
truly mean to you?
Does the trail through the woods
bring about rapturous
(oh how often I use that word)
far-gotten
childhood emotions?
Does it connect you to another state,
does it bring you upward,
does it refresh your tired soul
and replenish the achy corners
of your humanity?

Me neither.

Good.

Yeah, I'd love another beer, thank you.
But hey,
you want to go
to the park?
They're playing an awesome smut film.

YES

There was a time
before now
before then
much, much earlier than you're thinking.
No, before that.
No, sweetie, before that.
Earlier.
Earlier!
What part of earlier
did you not understand?
No, before that.
Keep going.
No, the time I'm thinking
came much before that.
Closer,
closer,
red hot,
Yes, that's the time.

Wait, what did you say?
No, no, I'm sorry.
Before that.

MEN AND THERE CURIOUS VICES

I caught you staring at me,
stranger.
You know the rules
according to New York bylaw 1128.
Stand up,
turn around
bend over
grab your ankles
and give me your best
choo-choo train impression.

Yeah, that's it.

IN ALL GOOD FAITH, THE TRAINING WILL START LATE

Keeping in mind all that we've learned here today,
Who would like to perform the first autopsy?
Come on, it won't kill ya.

Sorry, that was in poor taste.
Look, in this job, you gotta keep things light.

Now, who wants to gut this fish, eh?

What is wrong, Mr. Thomas?
Oh, good Lord.

No, Mr. Thomas, I don't think your mother's corpse
looks like a fish.
How the hell did you get into this section, anyway?
Having you learn an autopsy
on your own mother
seems like a sharp conflict of interest.

Oh.
Well, bad luck can sure be shitty, can't it?

Yes, Kelly, come on up.
Mr. Thomas, you may want to leave the room.

Good.
Now, let's have some fun, eh?
What should we draw on her stomach
before we slice her open?
I'm always partial to a sideways mouth.

HEM AND HAW AND HEMHAW

In my room
the fan has a celebrity's picture
posted on the front of it.

I am a fan of irony.

THE LAST INTROSPECTION

You've come a long way, haven't you?
You've crossed the plains
and took to riding trains
the hunger that daily riddled you
the dream of something you couldn't put to words
the dirt under your fingers built upon itself
the stars you counted every night
and the figures you dreamt you saw in them
and remembered what your parents told you about them
when you were a young one.

The stories you heard and the ones you told
the rocking of the car and squeaking of the brakes
your feet dangled off the edge
and you smoked rationed, careful cigarettes
most nights you were cold
and with no socks
and were forced to hide from authority flashlights
but you're young and you giggled at them
and danced around the dangers and verily taunted them.

You found routine in the open country
and laughed through your difficulties
and when your tooth fell out you showed everyone
and threw it out the rapid door
and showed them the blood on your fingertips
and nearly fainted before you finally chewed your shirt.
The dirt piled thick on your cheeks
and the smell accumulated in concentric circles around you
and grew through its own diameter.

You stared out at the black night
and thought about the uses of your fine arts degree
fantasized how they would all come rushing
how they would all see soon enough
just how brilliant and special you were
but not yet
for you wanted to ride the rails and see the world.
You sat cross legged and slept on bales of hay
and when you ear started hurting

you simply sucked on your pinky and cleaned it deep
and when it kept on hurting
you just ignored it.

You took to drink because the old guys told you to,
but never enough to regret it.
You kept your position
and stayed in the middle
and never leapt from your pedestal
and rode on and on.

The country is of course
oh so fucking beautiful.
And you've seen it all.

But now,
you're in New York City,
and no one gives a fuck
how fresh the air in Idaho is.
You need to fix that gap in your teeth,
take a shower,
and get your bleeding ear
seriously examined.

Because you have one week on my couch.
After that, I'm calling Mom.

Damn it, I'm late.
Don't touch anything, okay?

THE TIME-TESTED METHOD OF NUMBERING YOUR CHILDREN

Neil Young rocked in the free world
while an old man on a porch
somewhere in Kansas
simply
rocks.

CUPID'S TERROR

Hiding behind the vague curtain of twirled style,
that is the most prevalent quality.
When words have lost their substance
and deal only in misleading intentions and
black hole ideologies,
then the fashion of the time
has imprinted itself over again on willing participants
when the vacuum, the void, and the system
have all become one
and no longer do the lights turn on concurrently
and neighbors ask one another
what they really meant,
when imaginary conversations sway opinion
when plotting becomes a daily requirement
when what is said is only what is said
and not what is intended to be accomplished
when glances are worth millions
and hugs only pennies
the limitless nature of these intricacies
age fiercely and sweetly
and we are turning upon ourselves
and the look cannot be contained by one
and the ship steers itself into the fog
willingly
and the screams and shouts from those above
do nothing to deter the course
and new land is somewhere on the horizon
we are promised
we are assured
we are locked in tightly, sweetly, comfortably,
and there is no common ground anymore.
We are spinning in independent circles
and the time is going quickly
and the fields are all empty
and reading requirements lessen
and everyone is a
fucking comedian these days.

NOT ENOUGH SPACE BUT PLENTY OF BACON

It's two in the morning
and I wake up up
and because I never wake up
I think it's time to get up.
In the moonlight I check my watch
and see what time it really is.

Three more hours
is the most glorious phrase
I've ever been able to tell myself.

I should quit smoking
more often.

TOO COMPLETE

There is no awkward anymore–
We are away and done with it,
Tired of its presence in the exits
of social outings.
No more escapes or excuses
stuttering or constantly reflecting
always looking back–
we should press forward already!
Look to the future!
There is no awkward–
only opportunity.

I have a hairy chest,
and that in itself is an opportunity.

THE GREATEST PUN

A fisher of men
needs not bait–
just *hookers*.

DELIVERY DELIGHT

You have a weekend.
You have a newspaper
waiting for you this Sunday morning.

And I'm walking in your halls
with a job to do.

ALMOST COULDN'T SAY IT TO HER

In the back of a trendy antique store
There was a painting
in which a man
wearing an old suit
his back to the perspective
sat alone at a desk
holding an old parchment
and writing something
and the drapes in his room were closed
and he was on the left
and far off to the right
was an open door
to the outside
and the colors became bright out there
and there was sky
and some wispy clouds
and you really want to know
what the hell is he doing inside
and/or
what the hell is that door doing open?

It cost four hundred dollars,
so I simply remembered it,
left,
and then wrote it down.

Right now I'm thinking about
repainting my room
and re-learning the piano.

A MOMENT IN A POND

Imagination stretched
is nothing more
than willpower restrained.

This is the kind of thing
that Oscar Wilde might say
and then everyone would
feign
and swoon
and say oh how *true* that is
we are indebted to you
you are so witty
and entertain me so
and write the finest plays
and though I may not fully
understand
that little aphorism
I am *sure* that it is true
and I shall apply it to my daily life
and will learn from it.

Then they threw him in jail
for being homosexual.

REMINISCENT SUMMER'S SOUL

Tiptoe
through
the
window,
just don't wake the cats.

JEALOUSY

When the chips are down,
like really down,
like by your ankles down,
it might be time to sell.

IS THERE ANOTHER BUTTER PAD?

If there were a proven way to close it down then I would have no trouble doing so but since there are all these conflicting arguments and opinions on the matter that conflict with me and your personal convictions than we're just going to have to do it the way that our forefathers taught us when they etched the rules onto a stone tablet and passed it through the ages of secret societies through our fathers and finally down to us, the keepers of the secret. So when they ask you what happened to the lab and what became of the rubies and most especially to the documents you're going to have to lie your ass off and tell them what you think they're going to want to hear about it all even if it directly conflicts with something that you said only minutes previous to another enquirer and especially if you're talking to someone from the direct lineage because even though you and I are the appointed keepers the alliance could still have our balls in a vice if they ever found out the truth about how we handled the dismantling the burying the burning the fortifying the counterfeiting the relocating the manipulation the diverting the changing the rebelling. Because you and I are going to be the ones who change it all. Because you and I are meant to break this cycle. Because we know how wrong it has been and always will be. Because I knew the moment I first laid eyes on you in our respective chambers that we would rid the world of it all and they'd thank us for it but never even know it.

Because I'm in love with you.

NEWBORN

I am running a marathon today.
You know, they say that marathons
will make you impotent.
Wait, is that what they say?

THE SONG AND THE DANCE THAT IS NECESSITATED BY THE CLASS SYSTEM

It's easy to see where it comes from,
What's hard is seeing
Whether or not it is carrying a knife.

If it comes from
a long-forgotten
ex-girlfriend,
Fine.
It's coming from her this time.
Great.
But let us ask you this:
is she
in fact
carrying a knife?
Because that changes everything.

Maybe this time it comes from
news of a pregnancy.
Okay, fine.
You got her pregnant.
That's all well and good.
But let us ask you this:
is the baby,
inside that womb,
carrying a knife?
Because that
would certainly
change everything.

What if it comes
from an idea?
Fleeting, flitting, it usurps its way
into your imagination.
There you are in the park,
counting pigeons,
and suddenly you have it—
the problem solved, the solution so simple,
and you can't wait to go home and write it down.
What if the idea

[what, was holding a knife?]

No, I wasn't going to say that.

[Really? You weren't going to say that…]

Well, not exactly in those words.

[What words, then?]

I was going to say
that
what if the idea
were holding a knife?
Not *was* holding.
Were holding.

[…]

Seriously, though, *what if?*

CHRISTMAS

I have a list
and on that list
are the names of your family members.
How much do you want for it?

TULIP

Laying out in the sun,
the rays healing my every winter-gathered wound,
I am finally
at long last
in total peace.

This is
fucking
boring.

MIRROR, MIRROR

Why are you drinking again?

REPLACED BY KINETICS

Is there something on my neck?
Right there.
Because it feels like there is
something
on my neck.
Right there.
Yes.
No, not the mole.
No, not the tattoo either.
Right between them, actually.
I can feel it.

What?
Oh, it doesn't mean anything.
I got it in Asia.
Well, of course it means *something*.
Because I don't feel like telling you, we just met–
Look, is there something on my neck, or not?
No, I don't see the connection.
Because I asked you a simple observational question
And your question was a little personal.
I don't want to tell you what the tattoo means.

Oh my God, I can't believe you.

I think there might be something wrong with my neck.
Can you please just check?
I don't have a mirror handy.

Alright.

The baby is a symbol of my lost childhood,
you can see that it's missing its eyes.
It's riding a dolphin because

I've always had this strange feeling
that I'd be really connected to the ocean
even though I've never lived near one.
And the two of them
are jumping through a fire hoop
because I live a little dangerously.
The baby is reaching for the hoop
because as a child
I really liked playing with fire.
And they are both lit by a single spotlight
because I always felt
that I should have been a performer.

There.
Now you know.
Now you owe me
something about you.

Mm hm.
Mm hm.
Okay.
Wait, when?
Uh huh.
Uh huh.

Yeah, I have to go.

No, it's okay, I don't need to know.
I'll find a mirror somewhere.
No, really it's okay.
It was nice meeting you!

AMIGOS

Loving the life you have
is as simple
as pretending that your life
is a giant bowl of pudding.
And if your life already is that,
then,
well.

NOW, IN TIME, YOU WILL LOVE AGAIN

What does the wine remind me of?
Well, that's a citrus flavor
we're tasting,
and that takes me back.

There was a time
when a wine like this
would send me back
farther than I ever cared to go
back to my time as a lemon picker
and simply a-washing the fragrance in my nose
would be too much for me to bear
and I'd think of all the harsh whippings
and belittling slurs about my family name
and shouts from other immigrants
as they were seriously beaten
by the produce boss—

tasting a wine like this,
I would hear screams

as if they were happening again
and I'd begin to convulse and cry
simply at the thought,
the memory.

And it was once like this
that the smell of anything lemon
would bring me to an irrevocable state
and immediately
I'd then think about my escape
in the middle of that hot summer night
when the guards were too drunk
and I crawled through mud
under the barbed wire fences
throwing steaks I had a paid a painful price for
to shut up the dogs on the perimeter.
I would have run all the way home,
but it was too far
so I stowed away
in the vat of lemon rinds
that were on their way to the marmalade factory,
and I breathed through a tube

that stuck just above the rinds
for four days
en route to Alabama.

I ate lemon for sustenance,
shit my pants where I lay,
pissed to my left
and passed in and out of consciousness.
At a stop I finally was given the chance
to escape
and I ran
to the nearest bus stop
and telephoned Mom
to please let me come home,
and that I would explain later,
but Hal's Lemon Camp
was not what the brochures made it out to be.

What does the wine remind *you* of?

ORATE

Two hours ago,
I was on a ledge,
screaming for the fire department
to take away that damned jumper catcher.
If I was going to jump,
then jumping is *my* decision,
and I don't care
how messy
I make University Place.

You know,
I once read about a man
who lived on University Place—
I suppose that's why I chose
that building.
It seemed appropriate
because I knew about it
to splatter my innards
on that trash can.
I had it aimed and everything.
But of course NYC is a hotbed
of worry-warts
and someone saw me standing there
and called someone
and before I knew it
there were swarms of authorities below
and men on megaphones
and tourists with cameras
and young people,
those damned young people,
laughing and carousing
making obscene gestures,
smoking their cigarettes.

All I had wanted
was to jump in quiet,
unrecognized dignity.

So there I stood,
between a rock and a jumping rock,
wanting to choose neither—

and so I chose the flying rock.

I strapped on my hand gliding outfit,
grabbed the glider,
took a running leap
and caught a perfect wind–
swooping down over the pathetic hordes
like a superhero
I was weaving over traffic down University Place
down towards Washington Square Park.
I caught an updraft
and pulled up hard
and was thrust over everything.
I came out of the shadows
and into the beautiful sunlight
twisting with the wind
going where it willed
smiling among the silent skies.

I thought I'd had enough
and had better land
but I couldn't.
The winds built up
and soon I found that I was whisked
higher and higher.
The controls on a hand glider
don't do much
when the wind is so willing
and able.
I was pushed up
high above the clouds
and New York City
became a quiet dot
among an even quieter
dense, green, real-life map.

So now this is where I am.
Soaring higher and higher...
My hands are cold.
and now I'm beginning to wonder
about the amount of oxygen in the air.
Does it increase as you go higher?
I can't seem to remember.

1668

It was something about the way you talked
a tinge of sincerity that separated you from them
they were all talking about the business and whose work they loved
rambling on about the intricacies of the angles
and the past work that they had greatly admired
while sitting on their couch.

All of these words, these fables, these built-up fantasies,
all of them scraping to stay alive
none of them with anything but a resemblance of belief
with plenty of names to whip out at a moment's notice
who I couldn't possibly work with again
who I want to admire, aspire to
oh no I haven't seen that
have you seen this
all of us have seen
none of them have seen
I can't wait for that
for those two hours I get to sit on my couch again.

There was a time that I was once like you
I used to be on that same path as you
and surely if I hadn't jumped ship I'd be sitting there, too
because those ninety minutes used to be something special
I used to draw passion from them
they used to be so beautiful and pure
and then something happened to them
or maybe something happened to me
maybe I got too close to them
and they were always this way
this shoddy shallow demure manner
with which emotions and ideas and values
are so flippantly traded in conversation like playing cards
and the important parts are something else to those that run them
and the process is diluted from the original beauty
that spark of a flaming passion
(and even now— if there ever was one)
and it's pushed through the channels
and so-and-so says no
over and over again

and the end result is a far cry from the dream
and we're made to believe that it was the dream
and we're given inches from the bucket and call it a storm
and we're supposed to feed on it and draw from it
and eagerly we take it all in and are so meagerly satisfied
so dismally acquiesced
that we exchange and extrapolate things that were barely let through
and at the end of the day
we missed the sunset.

Don't let the insincerity of their voices
trickle down through you.

SATURDAY

If you give in that easily, son,
I'm going to tell your mother.
And you know how she gets
when you're all quitty.

So do it for both our sakes.

JUST DROP IT

I've been dizzy for the past couple of hours
and I can't figure what's wrong
So I tried staring at a Monet for a bit
and all that happened
was now I'm dizzy
and wow, those are pretty colors.

OKAY...

Oh my God.
Is that who I think it is?
I think it is.
He is seriously so great in that one thing he did.

Let's kill him.

THE INTRODUCTION

We are sitting in a hot air balloon
and circling the globe.
Here, here is a blanket.
I know it's cold, I'm sorry about that.
If you look in that wicker basket
you'll find cheese
asparagus
crackers
wine
and a few very good books.
Here, sip this coffee first.
This will help with the headache.

By the way,
I'm David.

FRIDAY

I passed a mirror this morning
and as I'm trying not to look at myself anymore,
I went to the proprietor
and calmly asked
if he could not put my image on display.

He said that as long as I didn't pass
in front of the mirror,
we'd have a deal.
I told him that this was a free country
and so I stapled a hundred of my headshots
all over his goddamned bodega.

PERHAPS AT NOON

There has to be more
than knowing lyrics to an obscure song.
Right?

No, there is not.
So get to memorizing.

OH, THE CRIMES OF OTHER MEN

I stood up in the class
and spoke my mind.

No boundaries
no fears
no pressure of peers
no glue on my lips.

Sprang forth from my lungs
a finer truth
such that my comrades
had never heard before.

I spoke
of wings on prehistoric animals,
of leering men in the backgrounds of historic photographs,
of religions only known to one man,
of the hygiene of Hitler,
of the theorems of the assistants of supposed geniuses,
of languages long forgotten yet still used,
of music everyone will get sick of,
of strange foods with stranger ways to eat it,
of footwear made from hand skin,
of not needing to be places
of time and place but not ever who,
of regret too soon and satisfaction too late,
of maladies strange and stingy,
of pleasures unsure and distant,
of knowledge lovely yet typical,
of hunger and its fictitious gains,
of net profit and corporate need,
of switcheroos,
of panting after a trip up the stairs,
of leaving behind a jacket,
of smells that only a rat could love
of the rocking of the 40's and the jazz of the 70's,
of movie stars long dead and unheralded,
of construction workers' hat sizes
of slippers rough and tumble,
of piano scales in reverse,
of the love of another,

of shoes and gloves,
of practice and patience and how it relates to honey,
of reflexivity and persistence,
of the dream deferred,
of Russian isolationist policies,
of Pictionary,
of needing to be right,
of tireless love-making,
of the cackling of the hyenas and the growl of the lion,
of suppositions and repossessions,
of The Beatles and their hotel room scandals,
of beaches far and true,
of the banging of the gavel,
of tunnels of love and dangerous consequences,
of endless wicks and everlasting candles,
of babies,
of the low and behold,
of tender chickens bred naturally and cage-free,
of nighttime eating binges in one's sleep,
of kindness from a bad Samaritan,
of hidden night clubs for Broadway's stars,
of fingernail pickings on the bathroom floor,
of rhinestones and their supernatural powers,
of kindness between brothers,
of enmity between sisters,
of indifference between parents,
of never being late,
of advertisement sublimates,
of uncertainty in the face of a proven structure,
of boats and parties and party boats,
of discounts on cheaply made furniture,
of capturing the essence of a mind,
of even numbers,
of improvised defense arguments,
of lines around the corner, all night,
of comparing yourself to others,
of tie-died bouncy balls,
of Christmas in July,
of the natural order of an ant hill,
of the wit and aplomb of British men,
of yearning for an apple,
of the extinction of the individual,
of gun control,

of music discordant and lazy,
of bald spots on old monkeys,
of sad moments in the life of a handsome devil,
of high-brow humor from a farting clown,
of well-thought travel routes,
of curly hair in the morning of life,
of easy-going, never-ending breathing,
of the miracle of water into wine,
of lots and having them,
of the right man for the job,
of equal pay,
of the nice time we had at the lake,
of clear visions and full heads,
of walking and seeing everything,
of really feeling new,
of this is my stop,
of the knowing of an obscure fact,
of the comfort level of bold individuals,
of wind,
of speaking out against the nations' drastically low water supply
of knowing the difference between ¾ and 1,
of skinned heads from prehistoric ages,
of the complacency of small animals,
of knowing where you're going part of the time,
of cream cheese and tomatoes on a bagel,
of visiting your sister etiquette,
of the imbalance of natural instincts,
of coming home early,
of plugs and chords and electronic missives,
of the thing! the thing!
of tasting the fruits of belabored efforts,
of looking over one's shoulder,
of looking over another's shoulder,
of the moment in question and the answer provided,
of sharp memory and dull pain,
of hypertension on posters,
of the anticipation of a fresh snow,
of mangled words and misinterpreted intentions,
of krill and fat,
of celebrity and the end of another boring episode,
of self-fulfillment,
of boxes upon boxes,
of spider webs and insects,

of changing your strategy,
of needing a mother,
of seeing a loved one complete a crossword puzzle,
of hoping this will never end,
of the dreams of running children,
of the present function of tuppence,
of thruppence,
of the comforting peace of exact numbers,
of the fluidity of feelings small and insignificant,
of those goddamned Germans,
of snickers and sneers from brethren-types,
of friends who work in recycling,
of caring about the environment,
of doing work for humanity,
of needing more focus and not knowing where to look,
of delving deeper for purpose,
of the incumbent,
of the needless display for fork-wealth,
of timers,
of not feeling at home,
of the retired,
of the dead and where they go,
of opinions,
of repetition,
of the inevitability of staggered desire,
of the bird's eye view of statistics,
of needing it, wanting it,
of what's the matter with you,
of matter itself,
of connections made and broken,
of reparations large and small,
of permanent tattoos on the souls of feet,
of pointing at the sky while the music swells,
of the gaudiness of language in excess,
of the what happened to publishers,
of the incessant stop,
of the wearing of a new beanie,
of time and its creepy younger brother,
of fuck the great turning of time,
of haughty art and lovely paintings at the museum,
of men with unbelievable talent,
of what to say to someone who loses,
of thanking everyone for being themselves,

of the innumerable people in our lives,
of spirituality and fake spirituality,
of the divine secrecy of the things that are good,
of the mysterious wonder of a pet's love,
of the peach,
of sweet delight in bakeries,
of holding hands but not hearts,
of the inversion of the frown,
of soft notes sung sweetly in memory's ear,
of a disturbing suspicion of unknowable events,
of utter hope,
of the swinging energy of together conversation,
of mistakes and are they really,
of complexes of the mind and retail fixes,
of acknowledging the the necessity of fierce, focused involvement,
of failing adjectives and appropriate nouns,
of simply too many nouns,
of never even having the chance to screw it up,
of Pilates on the decks of cruise ships,
of trips to the moon and dreams of the great beyond,
of the everglades and its inhabitants,
of buccaneers,
of running and its advantages,
of the time we went to the beach crammed in your white truck,
of sneaking away to the bathroom unbeknownst to your wife,
of learning and memorizing a truly great pancake recipe,
of the cast of characters that everyone, everyone can relate to,
of a cheap journal versus one with ponies on it,
of the organization of the mind on paper,
of no one has ever done that before,
of doing research,
of everyone criticizing your work,
of having your name attached to things,
of loving handwriting,
of needing to give up,
of commas and the elements of style,
of cafes, those wonderful cafes,
of higher learning!
of compatibility matched in the mind of your best friend,
of tinkering with the details,
of needing to see the sun,
of trying to figure out what may work,
of talking too loud,

of touching too much,
of appearing too eager,
of saying the wrong thing,
of offending someone who shouldn't care,
of side-stepping the point,
of polished or not,
of ready made and easily digested,
of long thought processes,
of seeing the real you in someone else,
of the bridges around the city,
of the history of comedy and tragedy,
of figures larger than life,
of efforts that may seem silly yet are later genius,
of everyone wants your life,
of eye contact in its billion variances,
of animal instinct on appearances,
of the past and present and absence of the future,
of afternoon sculpting classes,
of enrichment,
of writing seminars,
of poppy seed bagels,
of the bigger picture or the greater effort,
of who are you to tell me to research that specific point?
of confusion about teeth marks in the pudding,
of feline nap schedules,
of the editors of unheard of publications,
of the hidden lives of people you've only sort of heard of,
of the leather expression period in history,
of beats and rhymes and basic pleasures,
of fart jokes in vaudevillian style,
of skinny face,
of pleasure in place of pain,
of intuition and substitution,
of *Felicity*,
of naught versus not,
of the quiet time before sleep,
of doing this more later today,
of renegade words in forgotten books,
of panting and breathing for the first time in months,
of gunpowder plot,
of the solo shows of condemned artists,
of raised eyebrows and suggestive hand motions,
of saxophone pieces strewn about at the bottom of the ocean,

of losing one's tenure due to an illegal gambling ring,
of high voices that sound through the empty auditorium,
of nouns upon nouns yet again,
of the brevity of our aged fathers,
of green tea straight to the head,
of returned color and stricken pale sunsets,
of abandoned guitars on the side of the highway,
of morals true bested by those who seemed beneath you,
of intrepid individuals,
of money and its enticing allure,
of eating beans and rice every day when we were young,
of calling your father back,
of cleaning up for your girlfriend,
of remembering to drink water,
of old, heavy televisions,
of late night phone calls from someone you never really liked,
of still reading against all odds,
of pancakes large and small,
of the filthy urchins clinging to the bottom of the pier,
of the unbridled confidence of mentors,
of wanting to stretch out and intensify an argument,
of tense eye contact between amorous strangers,
of soft strokes between the thighs,
of reservations in popular restaurants,
of blank shirts bought in bulk,
of lightly inhaling a cigarette,
of being not just okay with gay,
of realizing, realizing, realizing,
of never considering your time wasted,
of beautiful curls unfurled in the morning,
of synapses fired at the sound of her voice,
of boots up to the knees,
of batted eyelashes,
of soft focus shot in black and white films,
of projecting your anger unfairly without noticing it,
of the overarching theme of justice in Charles Dickens novels,
of blue,
of flowers that smell like cars,
of synchronicity in termite inspections,
of love forsworn from professor to pool boy,
of the clanking of a fallen fork on a steel table,
of finally finishing the first page,
of re-realizing one's youth,

of the satisfaction of having been bold always,
of tough choices between dinner and bed,
of smooth skin and learning how to get it,
of wondering about the merits of Nirvana,
of tanning salons in beach towns,
of sunsets between long, thinning clouds,
of spontaneous drinks in bars with strange women,
of pensive times before nightfall with no music,
of never going back,
of the bullshit endured when trying to find truth,
of yes, Brad, this is me,
of multitasking even though the kids do it better,
of reason is the face of the beast,
of a bad back regretfully developed,
of moles and their peculiar placement,
of imperfection and the desire to fix it,
of never being able to,
of Cain and Abel,
of can-do attitudes when it will never can,
of peace talks with suspicious villains,
of knife-wielding babies,
of track lighting in Saddam's palaces,
of time spent with a book you end up hating,
of Washington's journey to the oval office,
of whatever happened to that woman,
of unexpected activities of brutish-looking men,
of settling the score,
of keeping track,
of taking your book with you to the bathroom,
of conversations with people halfway across the room,
of a purse full of thyme,
of rumors about the life of Danny Kaye,
of countless hours in one position,
of wondering about the secret,
of clenched fists around wrung up wet towels,
of smiling to yourself when no one's around,
of May and thank the Lord it's here,
of running around in circles and laughing,
of wondering why they do what they do in movies,
of hard work by everyone but exactly who you wished,
of it didn't take that long for us to get here,
of taking time off from everything,
of the overload of information and the quiet flow of thought,

of relationships— all of them,
of dribbling on yourself,
of mental ruin,
of physical care,
of tender tongues,
of the absurdity of life on paper,
of the timelines of each one of us,
of shifting in your seat,
of Frank fucking Sinatra,
of the crucible of Americana,
of the Cuba situation,
of crossing the border with a foreign fruit in your trunk,
of cross-eyed beagles,
of tried and true methods of interpreting a sneer,
of self defense with a spatula,
of drilling,
of loving your job, damn it,
of window wiping,
of it
finally
was
the
end
of
the
day.

Of course,
by that point,
the class had long already left,
lived their lives,
had children,
and died.

There simply is no such thing
as discipline anymore,
is there?

ERGO

It is nothing
It is a roundabout way of saying goodbye
this coming up with nouns and verbs
and then coming up with new ways of connecting them
so that each interaction, masked,
seems new and inventive and fresh.

We are clearly fooling ourselves
or else
we are all clumsy geniuses.

www.ingramcontent.com/pod-product-compliance
Lightning Source LLC
Chambersburg PA
CBHW020008050426
42450CB00005B/374